LAURIUM MICHIGAN'S EARLY DAYS

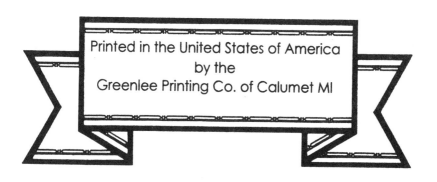

Printed in the United States of America
by the
Greenlee Printing Co. of Calumet MI

COVER

The cover photo was taken from a colored post card of Hecla Street in Laurium owned by Mrs. Isabelle Monette of Lake Linden. The picture was taken in about 1914, as this was the year when Hecla Street was paved and the town hall was rebuilt.

INDEX

AUTHOR'S NOTE

The data from which this book was complied were secured through numerous sources. From the many conflicting statements which appear in the original manuscripts and newspapers, this author has chosen the data and incidents which appealed to his reason, after all possible research, as being most accurate. If any errors are detected or important information missing, please contact me. These entries are a combination of many sources, most of which are listed at the end of this compilation.

Sincerely,

Clarence J. Monette
Author

The quiet residential community of Laurium is lodged in Calumet Township, Houghton County, and can be reached by traveling north from Houghton, on highway M-26. At one time this village was alleged to be the largest incorporated village in the United States due to its being next to the Calumet and Hecla copper mines, which lie adjoining and to the westward of it. Its population was 1,159 in 1890,and only twenty years later it reached its peak of 8,537.

Laurium could once be reached by four rail lines - the Mineral Range, the Copper Range, the Keweenaw Central and the Houghton County Traction Company. The Copper Range Depot was located on the east end of Third Street, while the Mineral Range Depot could be found on the corner of Third and Isle Royale Streets. The Keweenaw Central Railroad was also located at the east end of Third Street.

What is now known as the village of Laurium was originally the Village of Calumet. It was incorporated by the supervisors as Calumet in 1889, but was reincorporated and renamed Laurium in 1895. This was accomplished because the citizens wanted a post office of their own. Since Calumet already had a post office, the only way the community could get one was to change its name. Because the Laurium Mining Company platted the original Village of Calumet, a bill was introduced into the State Legislature to change the name to the Village of Laurium.

It also has been said that this town was named by its founders after or in commemoration of the mining city of Laurium (Laureium, in Attica), a district of ancient Greece. It is evident that the original fathers of one of the prettiest little residence and business towns of the Copper Country were students of ancient history. The Laurium in Greece commanded a district filled with rich mines of silver, silver-lead, manganese from ore, sulphur deposits, and great marble quarries. Copper was the important mineral at Laurium, Michigan. Since mining at the Laurium Mining Company was practically undeveloped, this venture turned out to be more of a speculative interest than obtaining a profit for its investors.

The Keweenaw Miner carried a story on April 22, 1916, titled "The Story of Michigan's Largest Village." According to the article, twenty-seven years earlier (1889) a few houses tenanted by some three-hundred people was organized and was called Calumet (now Laurium) Village. It stood somewhere east of the old Mineral Range depot and could be seen over the lumber piles of T. M. Lyon's lumber yard, but a few people said it was too far out to ever amount to anything. However, Red Jacket (now Calumet) was even in those days pretty well crowded, and people began drifting over to the new location, and soon the little village had a thousand inhabitants. Osceola Street was hailed as the coming big business street of the Copper Country.

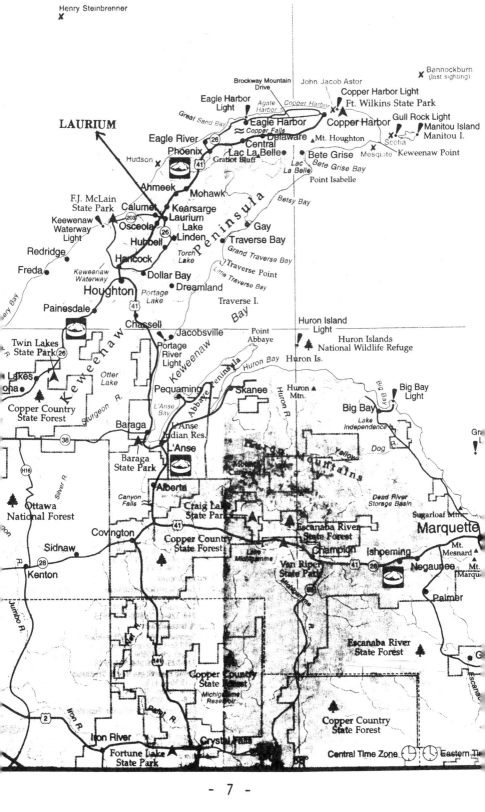

William M. Harris, the first president of the Village of Calumet, (now Laurium) went way back to Hecla Street and built a residence on the lot later owned by the Peninsula Plumbing Company store. R. H. Rickard also took a chance and built a residence on the corner of property later occupied by the Palace Hotel.

The newspaper article goes on to say that the village continued to grow, but Hecla Street, where the residences spoken of stood, was considered too far back for businesses. Osceola street was still the favored business thoroughfare. Johnson Vivian then decided he would branch out from his Osceola Store and erect a block in the village. Seeking a desirable location on Osceola Street, but finding property values too high, he went down to Hecla Street; and although at that time it was considered too far out, it was noted that within a couple of years Hecla Street had become the business center. Additions to the north and west were being built; and to help matters along, the street railway was constructed along Hecla Street, causing it to become a rival of Fifth Street in Red Jacket (now called Calumet).

At this time, the town had close to ten-thousand people. It had paved streets, fine business blocks, and mansions that would do credit to a city ten times its size. It had fine schools, including a Parochial High School, churches by the score, two strong banks, and a residential section that had no counterpart in the Copper Country. It still has a gas plant, and

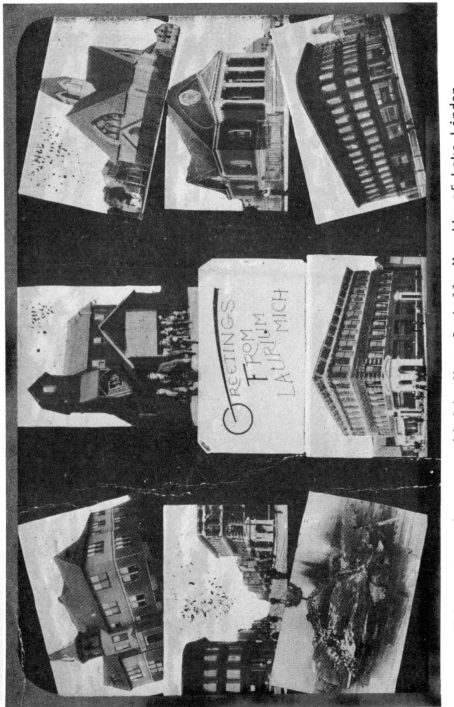

This post card was provided by Mrs. Isabelle Monette of Lake Linden.

used to be the northern headquarters of the electrical railway. This village had a very large proporion of the businessmen of Red Jacket residing within its borders, as they could not find room for their homes in Red Jacket which was wholly devoted to business houses.

Six blocks constituted the original village. They included the area now bounded on the north by First Street and originally known as Old Torch Lake Road, on the south by Fourth Street, on the west by Calumet Street, and on the east by Hecla Street. In the village's earliest days, Osceola Street was intended to be the main thoroughfare. Being situtated only about three-fourths of a mile from what was known as Red Jacket (now Calumet) proper, Laurium was quickly called a suburb of the town of Red Jacket.

Between the time when this village started as the village of Calumet, to 1895 when it was changed to Laurium, it was necessary to increase the area of the village six times. After the name of the village was changed, there were three more additions to the Village of Laurium. The area of the town was then two hundred seventy-eight acres and there were approximately eleven and a half miles of streets.

Mathias Sailer, John Mills, B. Venturino, Louis Gingrass, and William M. Harris were among the most active of those who directed their efforts towards the incorporation of the village. The first election was held in Jules Lamielle's home.

The first village election (under the name Village of Calumet) was conducted on May 14, 1889, and the first meeting of the Village of Calumet Council was held on May 16, 1889. At the first election the following citizens became officers: William M. Harris, President; Elburt D. Burgess, Clerk; Eugene O. Weldon, Treasurer; Jules Lamielle, Mathias Sailer, Martin B. Kuhn, Cleophos Therrian, George S. Wilson, and James O. Mills, Trustees; and Louis Mehrens, Assessor.

The following residents have served in the capacity of Village President through the years:

William M. Harris ..... 1889 - 1891
Elbert D. Burgess ..... 1891 - 1892
Mathias Sailer .... 1892 - 1894
George S. Wilson ...... 1894 - 1895
Frank H. Lathrop ...... 1895 - 1897
Joseph C. Light .... 1897 - 1898
Henry Filege .... 1898 - 1901
William L. Hagen ...... 1901 - 1902
Ernest Bollman .... 1902 - 1905
Paul P. Roehm .... 1905 - 1909
William J. Reynolds ... 1909 - 1911
Joseph Wills .... 1911 - 1916
Harry T. Ingersoll .... 1916 - 1919
John B. Cloutier ...... 1919 - 1922
Richard Edwards .... 1922 - 1925
J. B. Paton .... 1925 - 1930
Joseph Wills .... 1930 - 1936
Frederick J. Martin ... 1936 - 1943
Charles Salotti .... 1943 - 1948
Oscar F. Niemela ...... 1948 - 1948
Theodore M. Jacka ..... 1948 - 1952
Joseph M. Kline .... 1952 - 1960
Theodore M. Jacka ..... 1960 - 1962
Francis J. Cloutier ... 1962 - 1966
William H. Stephens ... 1966 - 1972

```
Glenn A. McCabe ....... 1972 - 1976
Kenneth J. Kangas ..... 1976 - 1978
Clement J. O'Connor ... 1978 - 1980
Frank J. Musich ....... 1980 - 1986
David A. Heinonen ..... 1986 - 1988
Kenneth A. Rowe ....... 1988 - 1989
Edward M. Vertin ...... 1989 - 1989
Walter Ala ............ 1989 - 1990
John Fontana .......... 1990 - 1991
Leonard W. Miller ..... 1991 - 1999
Mark L. Bonefant ...... 1999 - Present
```

Managers and Administrators

```
John Niemela .......... 1975 - 1981
David A. Heinonen ..... 1981 - 1985
Gary Auge ............. 1985 - 1991
Edward M. Vertin ...... 1991 - Present
```

As with other villages, Laurium had to enforce their cow ordinance. Seems that to curb the cow nuisance, village officials had been forced to take immediate action. With a view of permanently making an end to the stray cow problem, owners of bovines would be arrested under the village ordinance. Heretofore, a cow was occasionally impounded and a slight fee was required to recover the animal. The ordinance provided, however, that owners of stray cows would be arrested and a fine of $5.00 or more would be imposed.

By invoking this law, the services of a pound master would not be necessary and the move would be more effective according to Marshal James Wills to whom complaints of roaming cows had been frequently made. On the other hand, owners of cows insisted that pastures were not available and

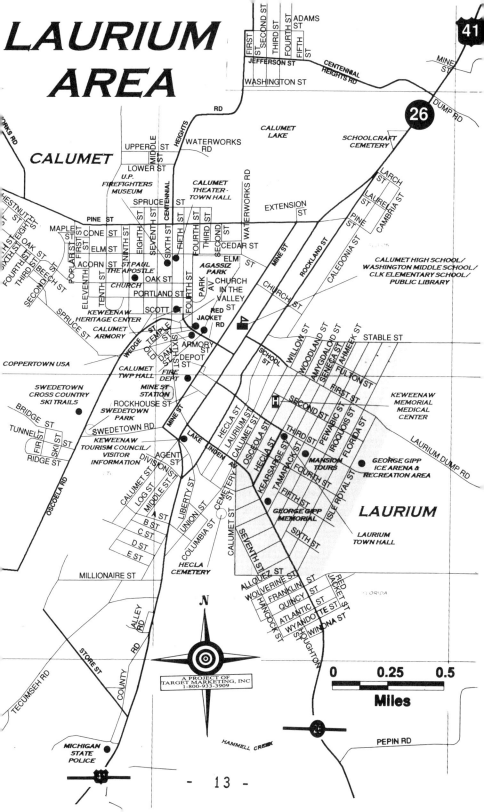

that until grazing land was opened, the cows would have to roam the streets. Notice was immediately served upon owners of the cows and of the enforcement of the ordinance. It was believed that would be sufficient to convince the owners of the stand of the police officers.

It may be worthy to note here that the village has never maintained a public school system. At one time the schools in the village, all a part of the Calumet Public School System, were the John Duncan, Charles Briggs, Horace Mann, Sacred Heart (both grade and high schools), Hawthorne, Irving, Holmes and the German Lutheran and Commercial School.

Incidentally the Holmes School was located at Lake Linden Avenue and Florida Street. It was one of the many schools that the Calumet and Hecla Consolidated Copper Company had built for the children of its workers. Built in 1898, it resembled most of those in the various locations.

The Holmes School located on Lake Linden Avenue, Florida Location, a wood-framed building built at a cost of $5,000 was destroyed by fire on March 22, 1902. At 1 o'clock, shortly before the first bell, smoke was seen issuing from the register in one of the rooms in the upper story. The building contained five school rooms and was heated by a furnace in the basement. By some unknown manner the fire crept up the hot air pipe and spread out under the floor of the second story.

This picture of the Holmes School located on Lake Linden Avenue and Florida Streets was published in the Daily Mining Gazette on March 17, 1979.

The nearest fire alarm at the corner of Second and Osceola Streets was turned in and the fire departments were on the scene before the fire could be seen or even definitely located. There was no fire hydrant within several blocks of the school, and the Laurium and Calumet and Hecla Fire Departments were compelled to string out about 2,000 feet of hose.

A south wind was blowing with gale force and the firemen had to work like trojans to locate the fire as it ate its way to the open air and north end of the structure, which was soon in flames. The distance was so great from the hydrant that two steamers were coupled together to produce sufficient power to the streams of water being played on the building. The three Calumet and Hecla fire engines and the big Laurium steamer were all pumping to their limit, but with the high wind and the progress the fire had made it was utterly impossible to save the building.

During the 1902 school year, the five classrooms were presided over by Miss Anna Parmenter, principal; Miss Daisy McGinnis, assistant; Miss E. Goldsworthy, Miss Lillian Bastien and Miss Anna Retallic.

The structure was insured with the Faucett Agency for $3,500, $2,500 with the Continental and $1,000 with the Queen Agency.

The Charles Briggs School was built in 1907, and is located on the

The Charles Briggs School, located in Laurium, as pictured here in February of 1983, has been closed for a few years.

north east corner of Fourth and Pewabic
Streets. Briggs was the largest of the
Laurium schools, being constructed of
brick and having ten classrooms and an
office on the upper two floors. In
addition there were several basement
rooms available for special activities.

After the school was closed for
a number of years, it was in August of
1993, that the Laurium Village Council
decided it would try to sell the
building. Northern Consulants was
hired to do an engineering study and
found that the building was
structurally sound, despite several
stress fractures and roof problems.
The 64 by 43 foot area of the roof had
to be replaced at a cost of about
$15,000 to $20,000.

A special meeting was held by the
village council in September of 1993,
to sell the old school building to the
only bidder, Laurium resident Tony
Locatelli for $3,001.00. The Charles
Briggs School sign remained on the
building, and if the building was ever
torn down Locatelli would donate the
sign to a museum for preservation.

According to R. L. Polk's Houghton
County Directory, there was also a
school called the Laurium Commercial
School with J. Frank Reinier as its
principal. Located in the Richetta
Block on Hecla Street, they taught
courses in bookkeeping, shorthand,
typewriting, correspondence, English,
commercial law, and commercial arith-
metic. Special attention was given to
business penmanship and expert account-
ing.

The village still has a very large
number of costly mansions built by men
who had found copper mining a particularly lucrative form of investment.
Many of these homes continue to be well
maintained by the present owners.

The summer season of 1900 saw a
big building boom in progress in this
village. Building contractors of all
descriptions had made active prepa-
rations to meet the rush which came
with the advent of spring. The
greatest number of new homes was in the
addition known as Florida Location.
There was ample building room in that
section, although its one great draw
back as a residence section was its
distance from the business district and
other centers of industry.

The expected street car line had
caused many people to decide upon
"Florida" as a place of residence. The
road was to be put in operating
condition the next summer, making that
locality even more desirable because
its residents there would be brought
within easy access to the business
centers.

At that time, housing accommodations were a serious problem to many who
were employed at the several mines. It
was nearly impossible to secure
suitable dwellings, and the condition
was growing worse. Rents were too high
within a reasonable walking radius of
either of the big mines and only the
successful business or professional men
could afford to pay the high rentals
demanded for flats and dwellings near
Laurium or Red Jacket proper.

All the surrounding mines were adding slowly to their working forces, and consequently the already congested living quarters were being further overtaxed. The question "where can I find a house or rooms to rent?" was encountered daily. There were men living two to three miles from their work, and this distance had to be covered on foot since the street car complex was still not completed.

In speaking of the building prospects of the summer of 1900, a leading contractor said: "I expect to do as much if not more building this season than I have for two years past. Nearly all the contracts I now have are for dwelling houses for working people. Some of them are fine residence structures, but from their location it beats me how a man can walk to and from his place of employment. Should that street car proposition be announced as a sure thing for next summer I would have more building than I could possibly find men to complete."

Laurium also had its own airport at one time. Back in July of 1939, the newly constructed hangar at the airfield was dedicated by the Ira Pemberthy Post, American Legion, in cooperation with the Houghton County Road Commission, sponsors of the hangar. Eighteen planes carrying thirty-six pilots visited Laurium on their fifth annual Michigan Air Tour as part of the dedication. The hangar was constructed by Civil Works Adminis-

The Laurium airport was one of the favorite stopping places when this picture was taken during the 1940's. Courtesy of the Mac Frimodig collection.

tration and Federal Emergency Relief Administration labor.

The airport covered an area of one hundred acres, so with such a small space flight training had been limited. The hangar housed only three planes conveniently and the field, though of sufficient length for light planes, had been considered a handicap for the airport having only one thousand five hundred foot runways.

In May of 1941, the Board of Directors of the Calumet and Hecla Consolidated Copper Company approved the gift of four-hundred acres of land at the side of the Calumet-Laurium landing field. The airport, which now covered an area of five hundred acres was one of the finest of its kind in the Midwest. C. F. Winkler, of the Houghton County Road Commission; G. T. Murphy, president of the Calumet Chamber of Commerce; and Fred Martin, Laurium village president, went to Ishpeming to attend a special meeting of the U.P. National Defense Committee about this new venture. They believed that the airport could be made to fit into the nation's defense program on a larger scale and the local interests would make every effort to seek establishment of a permanent flight program in Laurium.

It was on July 29, 1937, that the area citizens viewed a flying armada of more than thirty planes, of virtually every size and description, making up one of the largest air tours ever held in Michigan. The planes had started landing at the Calumet-Laurium

airport the day before when the annual
Michigan Air Tour arrived for its
owvernight stay as part of its
statewide itinerary.

Hundreds of persons lined the
broad area of the airport as the first
ships came down. Members of Ira
Penberthy Post and American Legion
were on hand for escort duty, and
police kept the crowds back from the
landing strip to avoid accidents. The
Houghton County WPA band played a
stirring march program as the planes
glided down to the smooth runway on the
northernmost stop of their flight.

Cars for transporting the flyers
around the Keweenaw for a tour were
provided by the local American Legion
Post with the Calumet Chamber of
Commerce cooperating. A gala reception
was also held for the flight
participants when the Aviator's Ball
was held at the Laurium town hall. A
special program of dance music was
conducted by the Northern Collegians
modern dance band. Flags were
displayed in front of business
establishments of Calumet and Laurium
as part of the recognization of the air
tour.

Three separate agencies sponsored
the 1937 tour, those being the Michigan
Board of Aeronautics, the Department of
Michigan American Legion and the
Michigan Air Tour Association.

It was during February of 1941
that a progress report was made on the
local flying school being conducted at
Laurium's airport and the Isle Royale

Sands under the Civil Aeronautics Administration in conjunction with Michigan Tech University.

Milo Fontana was the flight instructor and manager of the Fontana Flying Service which was in charge of the flight training. The local training started during the fall of 1939 and the school's outstanding record in turning out skilled pilots, as well as its safety record, had been recognized by the CAA. Fontana's quota had been increased from 40 students, (30 in the primary and ten in the advance aerobatics course), to fifty. Mr. Fontana had also added night flying. The ground course was taught at Michigan Tech; most of the primary course training was handled at the Isle Royale Sands near the college in Houghton, and the advanced course was taught at the Laurium airport.

Six planes were now in use by the school and the hangar at the Laurium airport was taxed to capacity with the result that one of the planes was suspended above the others to accommodate all the planes.

Expansion of the airport onto the additional property would give it six runways, each a mile long. The longest on the expanded field would be a mile and a quarter long from southwest to northeast in a diagonal line. In a north - south direction the airport would be one mile long and three-thousand feet wide and in an east - west direction. on the north end of the field, it would be four-thousand two-hundred feet long and one-thousand three-hundred twenty feet wide.

The State Aeronautical Board had already been expanding the flying program into a permanent one. They were happy with the many features the local airport had, especially that it was particularly suited to winter flight training, and this feature was being stressed to the aeronautics officials. The airfield was used both for winter maneuvers by local flyers and by U. S. Air Force fliers from Selfridge Field. The U.S. Air Force planes were equipped with skis for landing on snow and ice.

Now abandoned as an airport, this property currently houses the Bicentennial Ice Arena. The runways were converted to farm land many years ago.

Several residents residing in Laurium in April of 1916, were listed in The Keweenaw Miner newspaper as early village pioneers.

One of the gentleman's name was HARRY T. INGERSOLL and his postoffice in Laurium. It was also mentioned that he was President of the Board of Trustees of the village. Mr. Ingersoll was born in Delta, Michigan on June 23, 1872, where he attended school. He worked at the store of G. P. Clark, and then saw service in the pay of J. B. Smith, who was a lumberman and merchant at L'Anse.

Laurium Village Census

1890	-	1,159
1900	-	5,643
1910	-	8,537
1920	-	6,696
1930	-	4,916
1940	-	3,929
1950	-	3,211
1960	-	3,058
1970	-	2,868
1980	-	2,676
1990	-	2,268
2000	-	2,126

In 1899 Mr. Ingersoll came to Laurium and secured a position with J. Vivian, Jr. and Company, who operated one of the largest department stores in the Copper Country. Through hard work he was advanced to the position of cashier. Village President Ingersoll was prominent in Masonic circles, being a thirty-second degree Mason and held membership in the Blue Lodge, Chapter, Council and Commandery. He was a member of the Modern Woodmen. He was married and had four children.

HARRY E. KING needed no introduction as almost everybody in the Copper Country knew this gentleman. He was a progressive businessman and one of those result-getters who was always on the move. He belived that it was better to do things than talk of them. First it was automobiles, then the Copper Country Choral Society, always getting results.

Mr. King was born in Calumet, educated in the public schools and when he left the classroom, Mr. King took up plumbing. He learned to handle tees, elbows, valves, sell pipe and lead and prospered. He moved forward toward a clerical post and in 1894 went into the mining company's office. Here he stayed 19 years and then resigned to take up the management of the Calumet Colosseum. As head of the big amusement enterprise, Mr. King stayed on the job for thirteen years.

Mr. King was a trustee of Laurium and stood high in the Masonic fraternity, having taken the

This early winter scene of Laurium was published on a post card. Courtesy of Mrs. Isabelle Monette of Lake Linden.

thirty-second degree. Besides the Blue
Lodge, he held membership in the
Council, Consistory, Commandery and
Shrine. Mr. King was married and had
two sons.

EDWARD P. BAST was a banker who
had spent seventeen years among the
money of his neighbors. He was known
as not spending his time behind a
mahogany-table, as he worked right in
the open, behind a plain wood oak desk
in the State Savings Bank at Laurium.
He was always busy, careful, cautious,
and courteous.

He was born in the Copper Country,
at Calumet, on February 10, 1873. He
learned his figures, history and other
subjects which were taught in the
Calumet School system, and in 1889 went
to work for the Calumet and Hecla
Mining Company, remaining there until
1895. That year he packed up his
suit-case and went to Buffalo, New
York, where he attended a business
college.

In 1897 the State Savings Bank was
established and Mr. Bast was given a
position with the new bank, devoting
his days to pass books, deposits and
what other things are required of a
bank bookkeeper. Promotion followed
his efforts and in 1902, he became
assistant cashier.

Mr. Bast was a member of the
Masonic Order, belonged to the Blue
Lodge, Chapter, Council, Commandery,
and the play-ground of Masonary, the
Shrine. He was married and had two
children.

JOHN B. CLOUTIER was a native of Three Rivers, Canada, and was born there on October 13, 1863. He passed his school days at Three Rivers and after completing his education came to the Copper Country, reaching Hancock on May 20, 1880. There he went to work for the Franklin Mining Company and held a job at the mine for two years.

In 1882, he changed his address and his business, moving to Lake Linden and taking up carpentry. After using wood-worker's tools for a number of years, he entered the employ of Alexander Etheier. He remained with Mr. Etheier for two years and accepted a position with the Vertin stores, where he worked for twelve years. Here he mastered the grocery business, from beans to baking powder.

In 1909, Mr. Clouthier opened a grocery and meat market in Laurium. In his store he learned much of the country, its people and their needs. Friends persuaded him to run for the Laurium Village Board of Trestees, of which he won.

Mr. Clouthier was active in Catholic fraternal affairs, being Chief Ranger of the Calumet Lodge of the Foresters of America and President of the St. John de Baptist Society. He was married and had eight children, five sons and three daughters.

JAMES RICHETTA was manager of four or five different business enterprises and a Village of Laurium Trustee. He was a leader among the

Italian-Americans of that bailiwick. Besides being a practical man of affairs, Mr. Richetta was a conservator of a group of businesses interests.

Mr. Richetta was born at Pronzalito, Italy, on November 7, 1877, and came to this country when a boy. In 1894 he arrived in Laurium, having moved from Calumet. He was employed for some time by the Calumet and Hecla Mining Company.

In 1900, he returned to Italy, remaining a year, and upon his return took general charge of the Richetta business ventures, which were many, and varied, including reality, undertaking, etc. He was also serving on the Laurium Village Board of Trustees.

Mr. Richetta was a member of several fraternal bodies and Italian organizations, among which were the San Martino and Garihaldi Societys. He was married and had three children.

WILHELM WAAS was considered a worthwhile citizen, a thrifty, conservative, property-owning gentleman who kept his eye on tomorrow and thought and acted for constructive purposes. He made his home in Laurium and was a member of the Laurium Village Board of Trustess.

Mr. Waas was born in Germany, on August 1, 1867, received his education in the land of his birth and came to this country in 1891. He remained in Chicago for a short time and then moved to Calumet where he opened the Tamarack Meat Market. He successfully managed

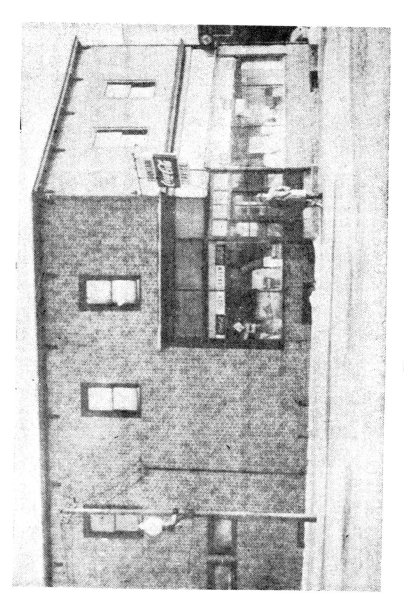

The Cozy Garden

the business a number of years before selling out. He then moved to Laurium where he opened the buffet.

Mr. Waas was active in fraternal affairs, being a member of the Sons of Herman, of which he had been state treasurer for seventeen years; German Aid Society of Calumet of which he was President; Order of Owls, of which he was a trustee, and the Loyal Order of Moose. Mr. Waas was married and had three children.

VINCENT VAIRO was one of the Italian-Americans who played a prominent part in the affairs of the Copper Country. Mr. Vairo was born in Locana, Italy, on June 22, 1866, and came to Calumet in 1890, working for the Calumet and Hecla Mining Company. After a successful record at the mine, he resigned to engage in the contracting business. He was one of the firms which held the contract for the erection of Laurium's town hall, and had also built many residences and other structures in this territory.

In 1910, he was appointed postmaster of Laurium and served until 1914. He was a member of several organizations and societies, including the Citizens League; the Alpena, Garbaldi and Christopher Columbus Societies. He was also a director of the First National Bank of Laurium. He served on the Laurium Village Board of Trustees. Trustee Vairo was married and had five children, two sons and three daughters.

Although the cornerstone located near the front door of the Laurium Town Hall reads "1914," this is not the date this building was constructed. It seems that on April 24, 1914, the Laurium village council decided that the town hall needed improvements and had architect Fred Maas prepare architectural drawings and plans. The remodelling was to take place that summer and bids for the work were requested. All bids had to be submitted by May 5, 1914, the date of the next regular meeting of the council.

It was expected that the bidding would be spirited as there was a lull in building every where in the country. Six or seven Calumet and Laurium contractors and builders entered bids, and the contract would be awarded to the lowest bidder.

It was on Wednesday evening, May 6th, that the bid from Chatel and Vairo Contractors for the sum of $7,990.00 was accepted by the Laurium village council. The work involved practically the reconstruction of the fire station, council chambers, the clerk's and marshal's offices, the dormitories and jail, and included the erection of a new sandstone front. A corrugated iron roof over the entire structure also was specified. In accepting the bid, the the council reserved the right to cut down the work and the contract price if it were deemed necessary.

A rather interesting feature of the contract was a clause which pre-empted the village from all liability

for accidents in carrying out the
remodelling plan. Although there was
no more danger of accident in work of
this kind than there was in any other
building work, the insertion of this
clause simply indicated that care was
to to excerised in taking into consid-
eration all possible contingencies.

All of the present building was to
be utilized, but a rearrangement of the
ground floor would provide more space
and a better location for the different
departments, while an addition to the
north side, thirteen feet wide by about
sixty feet long would eliminate
features which at that time were
objectionable. The addition would be
of sandstone, and the front would be
finished to conform with the front of
the old structure.

The addition would be two stories
in height to correspond with the
existing structure. The whole would be
given a front of cement plaster, which
would be very artistic, and a tower was
to be erected in front of the new
section of the building, replacing the
old belfry, which would also lend it
dignity. The crown of the tower was
four feet high. A big flagpole was
installed on the tower of the hall
where the stars and strips could be
proudly displayed. A fireproof wall
was to be constructed on the south side
of the building and would be completed
when the new part was completed.

The plans provided for a few
changes in the section of the building
which was used for the fire aparatus.
The clerk's office would be moved to

The Laurium Village Hall was rebuilt in 1914。

the front of the building, which was at
time occupied by the stairway, so that
it would face the street. It would be
reached from a hallway leading from the
main entrance. The change would
necessitate the building of a new
vault. At the rear of the hallway
would be situated the council chamber,
and in what is now the council chamber
would be located the jail, with the
marshal's office adjoining. On the
second floor of the new addition would
be located dormitories for the firemen.

Contractors Chatel and Vairo began
work on the town hall on May 18th,
1914. The contract stated that the
construction had to be completed in
ninety days. The initial step in the
$7,780 contract was excavating for the
addition to the north side of the
building. The addition would
necessitate the removal of the old fire
station and it was likely that the
building would be sold, if a purchaser
could be found.

An alteration in the contract
stated that the old sandstone, which
was removed from the gutters when the
cement walks were installed, would be
cleaned before it was used. Since a
considerable quanity of this rock was
covered with a black substance, due to
age and the action of the sun and
water, the stained stone was to be
cleaned by being treated with nitric
acid.

The steel columns used in the new
town hall arrived in June, and when the
wall on the north end was removed, the

This auditorium is located on the second floor
of Laurium's town hall.

supports were set in position. By this
time the remodeling of the interior was
progressing very satisfactorily and
most of the partitions had been
installed. The new vault had also been
constructed making way for the moving
of the clerk's office. The old hallway
which had lead from the front entrance
to the council chamber was converted
into a station for the hook and ladder
equipment, which was moved from the old
hook and ladder hall under the same
roof as the other equipment.

Work was also progressing on the
new council chamber which was located
at the rear of the clerk's office and
about the same size of the old chamber.
Behind this would be a small room for
committee purposes, and then would come
the marshal's office with a side
entrance and a door leading to the jail
room. The two jail cells which had
formerly been in the basement had
already been moved to their new first-
floor location. The new jail room was
a decided improvement on the old, being
far more sanitary and better venti-
lated.

At the front of the new addition
was a tower through which wound stairs
leading to the second floor. At the
base of the tower was a narrow hallway
leading to the council chamber and
clerk's office. The floor in the
front part of the building was also
raised to the street level, an
improvement that was considered very
desirable. The old hose tower that had
seen service since the hall was first
erected was demolished in August to

make way for a modern hose-drying device. One change in the original plan was authorized, namely the substitution of a steel beam for the wooden beam and supporting post in the council chamber.

With a view toward making the building throughly fire proof, metal laths were used and a sheet-iron roof was constructed. This was extended to the horse stables as well as the main structure and the result was one of the most modern buildings in the Copper Country.

The Calumet News carried a story on September 9th, 1914, stating that it was the intention of the village council to dispose of the old town hall, the building which was being temporarily occupied as headquarters of the village. The structure was to be sold and the lot converted into a grassy plot upon which, at some future time, a fountain would be erected.

Since everything was being built at a minimum of outlay, practically all the old furniture was used, and the only new equipment necessary was the filing cases for the vault. A new water heater was another convenience being installed in the building. In the past, the only supply of warm water for the use of the firemen, or in the stables, had been that in the fire engine, and that was very frequently not available.

The cornerstone was received in November of 1914 and was a thin sheet

of Vermont granite, beautifully polished and carved. The Council hollowed
out a niche in the corner stone of the
building at the base and to the left of
the main entrance and had the slab set
in. The slab contained the names of
the village trustees, president, and
executive officers.

During a meeting held on November
2, 1914, it was decided to move the old
fire hall building which fronted on
Hecla Street to the north of the town
hall to a site at the rear of the lot.
That would leave an open space for a
little garden plot and for a walk
leading to the side entrance of the
town hall proper. One section of the
building which was in poor repair would
be lopped off entirely, and the
structure would be moved a distance of
thirty-five feet. The building would
then be turned over to the firemen for
use as a club room and also for use by
the Laurium Band. The ground floor
would be used as a store-house for
village equipment. The Council had
invited bids for the purchase of the
building but none were satisfactory,
and its present location detracted from
the appearance of the town hall.

The Town Hall was dedicated on
Tuesday afternoon, November 24, 1914,
an event that had been long awaited by
the taxpayers and the general public.
The Council had arranged a reception to
take place during the afternoon, with
tours of the village hall, an open-air
concert, and brief exercises by Mayor
Joseph Wills and James T. Fisher. The
Laurium Orchestra also provided dance
music.

The villages of Laurium and
Calumet are also remembered for having
the last Catholic parochial school in
the two-county area. It was in 1887
that Msgr. M. Fauet devised plans for
the first parochial school in the
Sacred Heart Parish of which he was the
pastor. Because of some opposition,
these were abandoned.

Four years later, when the Fran-
ciscan Fathers from Cincinnati came to
the parish, the idea for constructing a
school was again revived. The initia-
tive was taken by the Rev. Peter
Welling, O.F.M., the presiding pastor.
Through his efforts, two lots on Lake
Linden Avenue in Laurium, were purchased for two-thousand five-hundred
dollars, and the new parish school
became a most welcome project. With
the zealous and generous cooperation of
the parishioners, the new school was
completed in the fall of 1891.

The teachers for the new school
came from the School Sisters of Notre
Dame. Laurium became a mission on
September 14, 1891, under the authority
of the Reverend Mother Caroline, who as
a Commissary General continued to
preside over all the American missions.
The first group of teachers consisted
of eight Sisters and one candidate.
The greatest interest and anxiety was
manifested in the Milwaukee Motherhouse
at the departure of the Sisters, as
Laurium was the most northern mission
at which the Notre Dame School Sisters
were stationed.

According to the Keweenaw Miner, dated September 2, 1916, the school was opened in 1891 with a registration of three- hundred and twenty-five pupils to whom the first Sisters were objects of curiosity, interest, and pleasure. Five classes were organized immediately, but owing to the daily increase in attendance during the first week, new quarters had to be provided during the second week, when the pupils numbered three-hundred seventy-five.

Eventually, as the school progressed, a high school course was introduced in 1893, when eight students, four boys and four girls, were graduated. According to the Daily Mining Gazette, they were as follows: Belle Monroe, Bridget Shea, Olive Waitkins, Nellie Tourangeau, William Foley, Michael O'Brien, Dennis Goggin, and Fred Kneauf. Lack of accommodations for the increasing enrollment soon necessitated additional room, and in 1902, Father Sigismund, a former pastor of the parish, undertook the erection of a high school building, at the cost of twenty-thousand dollars.

With the constant addition to the Sisters' community, their quarters became too limited; so in 1907, a new home of cement structure was built on the site of the first home. By 1916, the average registration of the school was about eight-hundred pupils, varying more or less annually.

They celebrated their twenty-fifth anniversary on September 17, 1916, with

The Sacred Heart Grade and High School buildings located on the corner of Calumet Street and Lake Linden Avenue in 1902. Courtesy of the Copper Country Historic Collections, Library Archives, Michigan Technological University, Houghton, Michigan

the Right Rev. Bishop Els and other
Catholic dignitaries attending.

All went well until 1953 when the
grade school building was condemned and
talk began among parishioners of
building a new grade school to service
all the parishes in the area. A new
school was built in Calumet, on U.S.
41, and the Sacred Heart Central School
was opened. In 1960, the Sacred Heart
High School building was condemned and
also closed. Thus ended the history of
the Catholic Schools in the village of
Laurium.

Laurium had a fire department long
before the village even thought of
changing its name to the village of
Laurium. According to R. L. Polk and
Company's Houghton County Directory,
printed in 1901 - 1902, the fire
department was located in the Town Hall
at 312 Hecla Street. The village then
had one steam fire engine, one hose
cart, and eighteen paid members. Henry
Vogler was the chief with Peter
Charrier as secretary and Martin B.
Kuhn as the treasurer. George Kuhn was
the first assistant, Thomas Archie the
second assistant, Fred Hohner the first
engineer, and John Stetter was the
second engineer.

LOCATION OF FIRE ALARM BOXES (1901)

Box 3 - Corner of Fulton and Iroquois
Box 4 - Corner of First and Hecla
Box 5 - Corner of Third and Pewabic
Box 6 - Corner of Fourth and Hecla
Box 7 - Corner of Tamarack and Lake
         Lake Linden Avenue

This picture of the Laurium Village Fire Department, taken in 1902, can be found the village hall. Courtesy of the Fire Department, Laurium, Michigan

Box 8 - Corner of Iroquois and Lake
        Linden Avenue

     Back in 1902, Laurium officials
were trying to improve their fire
protection. This was greatly appreci-
ated by property holders at the north
end of the town who for a long time had
been without adequate fire protection.
There were no hydrants close enough to
the newly built portion of the town to
insure them of much protection in case
of a bad fire, and there had been a
constant kick from the insurance people
and from the property holders who
wanted an improvement in the system.
The town expanded so fast in that
direction and the proposition of
extending the pipe system was such a
difficult one that it was some time
before hydrants were located in
Bollmann's additon. Even then the
houses were built so far out that it
would be difficult to reach some of
them from the hydrants.

     The Laurium officials had found
that in addition to the regular water
system throughout the city, their
cisterns had at different times saved
the property from destruction by fire.
The city had owned a cistern near the
corner of Third and Hecla Streets, one
near the Sacred Heart School, and
another near the corner of First and
Hecla Steets. These three cisterns
were large and located so that they
were of great value to the town in case
of fire. The council had also decided
to build another cistern, to be located
in Bollmann's Addition.

Seated, left to right—James O'Brien, Irving MacDonald, Oscar Holmstrom, Chief; Jack Torreano.

Standing, left to right—Henry Westphal, Rutherford Lowery, George Honold, William Stephens, John Baranotti, Frank Beaudette, Joseph Kline, Frank Torreano, Fred Sanders, James Richetta, Thomas Deegan.

Oscar Holmstrom, Chief; James O'Brien, Assistant Chief; Jack Torreano, Secretary; Fred Sanders, Engineer; James Richetta, Assistant Engineer; William Stephens, Assistant Engineer; Frank Torreano, Henry Westphal, Jack Barinotti, George Honold, Joseph Kline, Rutherford Lowery, Martin Herman, Stewart Solomonson (Armed Service), William Dunlop—Present Department.

This cistern was twenty-five feet wide by forty feet long and seventeen feet deep. It was located near the village limites on Fulton and Pewabic Streets and in such a position as to be of the most service in case of fire for which the hydrants would not help.

During the summer of 1906, the needs of the fire system for large fires had already been demonstrated when the supply of dam water was inadequate. The main reason for this was that the water mains were not all connected. When the village was first formed the system surrounding the town had a number of "dead ends" or places where the pipes were individual. Addition after addition was built and to each the water mains were extended, leaving more "dead ends." These would all be connected and the pond water system would be continous so that one engine drawing from a pipe did not exhaust the supply of water and rob another engine of this requirement.

It was on Thanksgiving Day in 1908 that the Village of Laurium fire department became the first department in the Copper Country to become equipped with an aerial ladder truck. It was purchased from the St. Louis, Missouri fire department for $3,350.00. If purchased new, it was estimated to cost $35,000.00.

Four members of the Laurium Department made the trip to St. Louis to pick up the truck and drive it back. The aerial ladder on the truck was 65 feet long and was hydraulically operated from a turntable on the truck that was about five feet off the ground.

In November of 1916 the Laurium fire engine which was small, compact and powerful, had to be shipped to the manufacture in New York to be equipped with a new boiler, the old boiler being leaky and rather unsafe. So, for about five or six weeks, or longer if necessary, the Laurium department used a big powerful reserve engine owned by the Calumet and Hecla Mining Company, which was one of the first fire fighting engines owned by the company and was one with a history.

The big engine was built to be hauled by three horses and then only on smooth city streets. In 1916, however, it had to be hauled by two horses, the three-horse equipment having been replaced because of the narrow roads in the Calumet district during the winter season. The engine was so large that it just scraped in through the doors of the Laurium fire station. Driver Sam Anderson of the Laurium engine team said that his team, although not the heaviest fire team in the Copper Country, could handle the big engine, either on wheels or ice runners.

The engine weighed six and a half tons, all brightly polished steel and nickel and copper. Its wheels were big and powerful enough to support a good sized locomotive. It was manufactured by the Amoskeag Company. Members of the fire department were informed that this big engine was used in the

historic Chicago fire in 1911 when the
big blaze swept through a great part of
the business part of the metropolis of
the central west, following the kicking
over of a lantern by a cow. It was
brought all the way from Boston to
Chicago to fight the blaze, for fire
engines were hauled in from cities in
all directions for that conflagration.
When the fire was put out, it was taken
back to Boston again.

Official fire department records
have been kept since 1894 and show that
the following men have served as
village Fire Chiefs:

Thomas Mills   - 1894 to 1903
Henery Vogler   - 1903 to 1906
Gust Preuss   - 1906 to 1934
Oscar Holmstrom   - 1935 to 1947
James O'Brien   - 1947 to 1959
Joseph Kline   - 1959 to 1963
Donald A. Julio   - 1963 to 1989
J. Michael Shaltz   - 1989 to 1999
Daniel Mukavetz   - 1999 to present

This department put its first
motorized pumper into service in May of
1930 and first used its booster tank on
a roof fire at the W. H. Thielman home
on May 27, 1930. The motorized ladder
truck was put into service in August of
1930. Still in service in this
department is the first motorized 1930
American LaFrance, 750 G.P.M. pumper.
This truck still runs, and the firemen
use it for all parades and other
celebrations. The pumper can be used
for a backup pumper in times of
emergency.

New fire trucks purchased are these:

A 1962 Ford Darley Pumper, 750 G.P.M. pump and 750 gallon booster tank. This truck was purchased in 1963 from Calumet Township and sold in 1983 to the Lac LaBelle Fire Department.

In 1968 they bought a 1947 aerial ladder truck from the City of St. Louis, and sold this it in 1983 to a local roofing firm.

In 1977 they purchased a new 1000 G.P.M. pumper with a 750 gallon booster tank from the Grumman-Howe Fire Equipment Company. This truck is still in service.

In 1983 the village purchased a 1966 John Bean combination aerial-pumper, with a Reo chassis from the Vails Gate New York Fire Department. It has a 65 foot aerial ladder and 300 gallon booster tank, ground ladder, hose bed, and compartments.

The fire department was moved from its home in the village hall to a building located between Allouez and Florida Street in Laurium. It was previously owned by the U.P. Power Comany and was no longer needed when they moved to the old Bosch Brewery property in Houghton. The move to the brick building with a concrete block addition was completed during the spring of 1996. Two large trucks are maintained in the concrete block building, those being the pumper and the new Quint (an aerial - ladder) truck which was purchased in October of 1996.

Some of Laurium's earliest societies were the Association of American Canadians, St. Louis De France Court number 46; Order of Owls; Calumet Social Club; AOH, Calumet Temple number 234; Hecla Legion number 1868; Ho-on-kee Rod and Gun Club; Young Men's Catholic Club; Calumet Maennerchor; St. Jacobs Austrian Society; Sampo Tent number 626, and Wellama the Temperance Society.

Some of the Italian Organizations were the Legione Federale G. Garibald, Loggia number 61; Saint Jacob's Society, and the Societa Ettore Perone Di San Martino Canavese.

Other organizations include the Knights of the Modern Maccabees; Ladies of the Modern Maccabees; Knights of Pythias; Pythian Sisters; Modern Woodsmen of America; and the National Protective Legion.

Most Copper Country villages had a horse track, and so did Laurium. In December of 1906 a local newspaper notified its readers that the new speedway in Laurium had been completed and its first exhibitions were now under way. Several of the fast horses had been given trials upon the track and officials promised that it would be kept in the best possible condition.

It was noted that the support for the work came from those who had fast

1919-20 students from the Laurium Commercial School. Courtesy of the Lauri W. Leskinen collection.

horses, and that there was no revenue from the public, so every encouragement should be given to the owners of the fast horses. There were a number of fine races conducted on the speedway and new horses were brought to Laurium for the sole purpose of winning the title of champion of the district.

Postmaster Charles Wickstrom and James McClure brought horses to participate in the races. Owners of horses in Hancock, Houghton, Lake Linden and other towns were invited to come here and take part in the matinees.

It was reported that on the Fourth of July of 1908 an excellent card of races was pulled off at the park. The finest and fastest nags in the Upper Peninsula entered the races, being from Marquette, Ishpeming and other Iron Country towns. Included were horses from Hancock and Calumet, with entries from one or two Wisconsin towns. The field was completely fenced and grandstands finished. A couple of running races were included and a free-for-all in the pacing and trotting was held.

As mentioned before, it was in 1895 that the residents of this community wanted a post office of their own which caused the Village of Laurium to come into being. Thomas Buzzo became the first postmaster on February 28, 1895. The post office was author-ized to issue money orders on June 11, 1895. The office operated indepen-dently until December 31, 1935, when it

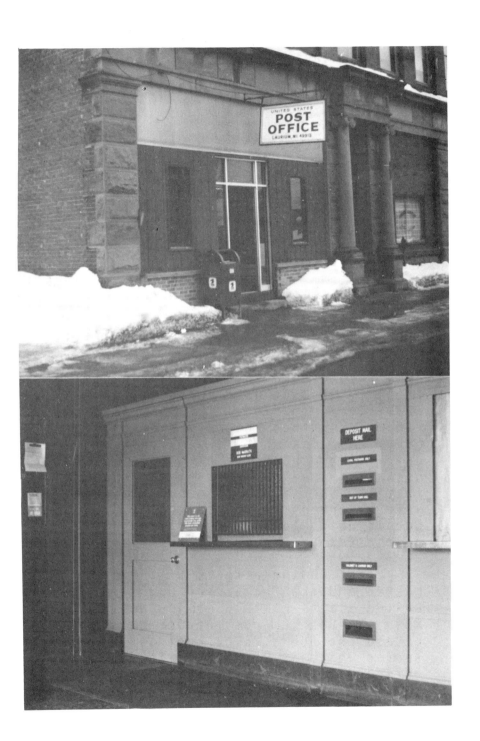

became a branch of the Calumet post office. Since that time a Clerk in Charge has been appointed to take care of the branch, with the current clerk being Robert L. McGrath.

During the past few years the branch post office at Laurium has had its problems. The Postal Service wanted to cut costs and had a survey done which found that the Laurium facility was not used enough to warrant full-time operation. It was recommended that the office be open only from 11 a.m. to 1 p.m. on week-days. These hours were posted, but a canvas of area business firms concluded that the shorter hours could not satisfy the needs of the community, according to Terry Cardwell, who was postmaster of Calumet at the time.

Through the efforts of the post-master and the Chamber of Commerce, the United States Postal Service decided to keep the Laurium post office open and extend the hours. The postmasters who served while it was a full-service post office were:

POSTMASTERS:	DATE COMMISSIONED:
Thomas Buzzo	February 28, 1895
Matthias Sailer	March 1, 1901
Robert C. Faucett	February 23, 1905
Nannie Faucett	April 23, 1906
Vincent Vairo	April 20, 1910
John A. Gries	February 4, 1928

The original Calumet Public Hospital was established in 1903 and was situated on the corner of Third and Florida Streets in Laurium. This was a non-profit corporation, and the building was originally constructed through private donations and subscriptions.

The structure consisted of a large family dwelling with a bed capacity for twenty persons. It served an area that extended to the tip of the Keweenaw Peninsula and as far south as its patients hailed from.

It was during December of 1905 that the residents of Laurium had to deal with a scarlet fever situation. For the past eight weeks, Dr. D. K. McQueen, health officer for this village, who also had charge of most of the cases in that village, stated to a Daily Mining Gazette reporter that the danger of an epidemic had been greatly reduced, and that the chances for the complete eradication of this dreaded disease were more promising.

Scarlet feaver had become quite prevalent in this district about eight weeks prior. Laurium seemed to bear the brunt of the disease, the fever

being practically confined to this
village, except in isolated instances.

Since the first case was
discovered in Laurium, there had been
eight deaths from the scarlet fever,
all being confined to children. As in
accordance with the provisions of
burial in cases of scarlet fever
interment in almost every case took
place within a few hours.

The only adult who expired as a
result of scarlet fever was Dr. Louis
Gelston, internist of the Calumet and
Hecla Mining Company hospital in the
neighboring village of Calumet. Dr.
Gelston contracted the disease while in
attendance of scarlet fever patients.
He was taken to Kalamazoo for
interment.

As of December 28, 1905, there
were still fourteen homes under
quarantine in the village of Laurium,
with thirty cases keeping the physicans
busy. This was a decrease of about
twenty cases in the past two weeks.

It was hoped that the schools
would be able to resume their sessions
after the holiday vacation without any
fear of a further spread of this
disease.

In 1908, a Nurses Training School
was established in the Hospital. In
1918 the name was changed to the
Houghton County Training School for
Nurses and their course of instruction
took three years to complete. Nine
months of this time the nurses were

affiliated with a Detroit hospital, with three months spent in pediatrics, three months in Contagion at Herman Kiefer, and the remaining three months in women's obsetrics. This obstetrics. training school was discontinued in 1932.

In 1920 and 1921 a new twenty-one bed hospital was built on the corner of Second and Osceola Streets, and the old hospital was closed. This new structure was financed through generous donations from Mr. Gordon R. Campbell and Mr. Thomas Hoatson. A private drive was also conducted to raise the remaining funds. The old Calumet Public Hospital building had become inadequate and had outgrown its use as a public hospital. The structure and equipment lacked the ability to handle the large number of patients which had been confined to it, and the number of patients was steadily increasing each year.

This institution was built as a memorial to the soldiers and the sailors who died in World War I. In 1919 a local newspaper reported that at that time there were only four hospitals in the district, and this was the only one open to the public. The other three were owned by mining companies and were solely for the use of their employees and their families. These three hospitals were the Calumet and Hecla Mining Company Hospital, the Mohawk Hospital, and the Lake Linden Hospital. Throughout the years, the corporation name has always remained the Calumet Public Hospital.

In this second building, the nurses' quarters were in the south end of the building. This later became the obstetrical and x-ray departments when Dr. Laubaugh died in 1923. At this time the doctor bequeathed his home on First and Willow Avenue for use as a nurses' residence. Miss Emma Petermann was housemother to the nurses until the closing of the training school in 1932.

The clinical laboratory and x-ray departments were established in 1924 with Mrs. George Unsworth being the first laboratory and x-ray technician. Mrs. Joseph Vertin donated the first x-ray machine to the hospital as a memorial to her husband.

During 1950, a small addition, known as the Dr. Donald K. MacQueen Memorial Emergency Room, was constructed for first aid and minor emergency surgery. Within a short time it was converted into a ward to provide additional bed space.

The board of trustees were well aware of the overcrowded conditions in the hospital, when in 1958 they hired the administrative head of the Chicago Passevant Hospital. He was a recognized authority on hospital planning and layout and was to make a study of further expansion. He advised the trustees to construct a new hospital.

Due to limited resources, a new maternity wing was designed instead. A building fund of over $60,000 plus a grant from the Ford Foundation in the

ET PUBLIC HOSPITAL, LAURIUM, MICH.

The original Calumet Public Hospital building at Third and Florida in Laurium

amount of $22,500 help set the wheels
in motion for the construction of the
new wing. The hospital also had a
trust fund for maintenance and the
replacement of equipment. It also
covered operating expenses during slack
periods when the hospital inevitably
operated at a loss.

The new wing was eighty-eight feet
by twenty-eight feet and consisted of a
basement and first floor. It was
dedicated on May 12, 1959, which was
also National Hospital Day. That day
was also set aside to commemorate the
birthday of Florence Nightingale, the
first training nurse.

The new maternity ward was
designed to comply with the standards
set by the Michigan Hospital Association. It had three and five bed wards,
a nursery equipped for eleven infants,
labor and delivery rooms, a doctors'
scrub room, lavatory, and a nurses'
facility room.

The basement housed the kitchen,
maids' dining room and storage rooms.
Peter Locatelli of Laurium was the
construction foreman when the ground
was first broken. The wing was
completed on April 30, 1959. Lumber
and building materials were provided by
the Armstrong Thielman Lumber Company.
Al Wickstrom and Associates did the
carpentry and finishing work while
Hermann Hardware was in charge of
plumbing and heating.

Calumet Public Hospital — original building constructed in 1920. Courtesy of the Daily Mining Gazette, Houghton, Michigan, October 29, 1983.

Electrical supplies and fixtures were provided and installed by the Taylor Electrical Company. Ceramic tile, floor tile and linoleum were furnished by the Dollar Bay Linoleum and Tile Company. The Calumet Division of the Calumet and Hecla Mining Company donated a special oxygen type Wolverine copper tubing. This was installed by Markus Martimaki of Calumet. In 1963, a seventeen-bed addition was opened on the second floor at the north end of the building. This was completed at a cost of $78,000.

New construction work began in October of 1964 when it was decided to have a expansion and remodeling program. A $400,000 bequest from the will of Joshua Daniell and the donation of time and money from the hospital auxiliary with the assistance from the people in the region, made possible for the new highly modernized facility. The $450,000 added a new wing to the structure and increased its bed capacity to seventy-seven. It also provided a large number of new and improved services which made use of the very latest in hospital equipment.

Much of the new addition was devoted to administration and special services. These included an enlarged x-ray department, an entirely new laboratory, two new operating and emergency rooms, and for the first time in the hopsital, a morgue.

The basement was changed into a spacious and attractively furnished lounge, and the new entrance now leads directly to the admitting, administration, credit, library and record offices.

A new elevator lifts the staff members, patients, and visitors to the hospital's four floors. Solariums equipped with televisions, stuffed chairs, and sofas and featuring floor to ceiling windows with a southern exposure, were constructed on the third and fourth floors. Patients and visitors welcomed these pleasant meeting places.

The staff was also very pleased with the new closed circuit television with its fluoroscopic image intensificatiion x-ray unit. This is typical of the quipment that is now being used throughout the hospital.

The hospital also has an Auxiliary which is in its thirty-eighth year. It has thirty-five active members who sew, mend, and wrap dressings. The estimated value of this donated service alone totals in excess of $10,000 yearly. Each year, in November, the Auxiliary conducts an annual membership drive. With the generosity of their supporters, they are able to purchase equipment for the hospital.

According to the Daily Mining Gazette dated March 25, 1982, this hospital is the second largest employer in the community. It was a seventy-bed hospital, with about two hundred thirty-five full- and part-time employees (the equivalent of about one

hundred sixty-five full time
employees), representing a yearly
payroll of two and a half million
dollars.   Since 1982, the hospital
staff has seen a new computer system,
new patient heart monitoring devices in
ICCU, new surgical equipment, new
nuclear medicine, and x-ray and ultra
sound equipment among other things
added to the hospital's facilities for
health care.

**CALUMET
PUBLIC
HOSPITAL**

205 Osceola Street
Laurium, Michigan 49913
(906) 337-3100

    Laurium is known for the legend of
George Gipp. This lad, who became
Nortre Dame's first All-American, lived
but twenty-five years and has been dead
for more than twice that long. Yet the
mention of his name sparks the same
recognition among sports fans as does
Red Grange of a bygone era or Joe
Namath. Gipp has been enshrined in the
National Football and Michigan Halls of
Fame and more recently in the Upper
Peninsula Sports Hall of Fame.

    He was born at 432 Hecla Street,
in Laurium on February 18, 1895, a son
of Mr. and Mrs. Matthew Gipp. Gipp's
untimely death came in his senior year

at Nortre Dame when he was at the
zenith of his colorful sports career.
Participation in sports brought him
instant immortality after a few short
years of football glory. What Gipp's
fate would have been had he lived
longer provokes only pointless thought.
The sport writers of his day, including
Grantland Rice, described The Gipper's
play as so uncanny and his skills so
natural that it's reasonable to assume
that he would have starred in profes-
sion football.

Gipp attended the Calumet public
schools. It is reported that he never
played high school football. He was,
though, an all-round athlete, joining
in sandlot football, baseball, track,
and hockey. Joe Mishica recalls Gipp
as being a friendly kind, and very
personable to everyone. Mishica
recalled that one of the main reasons
he never played football for Calumet
High was that he preferred playing pool
after school rather than going to
football practice. He'd head right up
to the pool hall, which was located
where Mullen's Dry Cleaning is now. It
was as a college freshman that the six-
foot, one-hundred-eighty pound Gipp
drop-kicked a sixty-two yard field goal
against Western State Normal. The kick
is one of the longest in collegiate
history.

In his four-year, thirty-two-game
college career, the Gipper scored
eighty-three touchdowns while the
Fighting Irish won twenty-seven, lost
only two and tied three. In his last

twenty games, Notre Dame won ninteen and tied one, scoring five hundred six points to their opponents' ninety-seven.

A 1961 Gazette story noted that Gipp probably would have lived much longer had he heeded the advice of the late Dr. Andrew C. Roche of Calumet who wanted to remove Gipp's infected tonsils in the summer of 1920. Gipp said he would have them taken out when he returned to school in the fall. He never did - and contacted streptococcic infection of the throat in the Illinois game on November 20th.

Gipp's last game was against Northwestern at Evanston, Illinois. Suffering from the infection plus a painful shoulder injury, he was forced to remain on the bench with his throat bandaged through the early portions of the hard-fought contest. Northwestern was ahead by a few points but when Nortre Dame neared the Wildcat goal line the partisan crowd began a taunting chant of "Bring on your mighty Gipp!"

Coach Rockne let the pleading Gipp enter the game. On the next play, Gipp silenced the chant when he took the ball and drove for the touchdown. He stayed in the game until Notre Dame built up a substantial lead, then walked nonchalantly off the field. Gipp was later hospitalized and died at 3:27 a.m. on December 14, 1920. He was buried in Calumet on December 18th with military rites from the old Calumet

GEORGE GIPP。 Courtesy of the Daily Mining Gazette,
Houghton, Michigan. Saturday, September 5, 1981。

Lightguard Armory. Laurium and Calumet stores closed for the funeral.

Citizens of the Village of Laurium built a memorial to the Gipper. This Memorial is located at the corner of Lake Linden Avenue and Tamarack Street, a short distance east of U.S. 41, the main artery carrying motorists to the Calumet-Laurium-Keweenaw area. On a well-manicured triangle of lawn and flowers, a large ten-foot concave stone structure to Gipp recognizes the man and his athletic prowess. The brass plate attached to the memorial reads "In memory of George A. Gipp, All-American, 1895-1920." In the center is the design of a football. His Mother attended the dedication ceremonies of the Gipp Memorial in 1935.

The George Gipp memorial located on the corner of Tamarack Street and Lake Linden Avenue, was restored during the summer of 1999. The memorial was now 64 years old and was torn down to make way for a new one that would be exactly the same, except that the fountain would work and that flowers would grow nearby during the summer. Laurium resident Jerry Vairo spearheaded the project. He noted that two Notre Dame graduates came to Laurium in 1995 and saw how the monument was deteriorating. The two graduates went to the Notre Dame clubs and members donated $100.00 or more to have an enscribed brick with their name put in a walkway in the restored park.

The walkway was not only the restored part of the park. A new fifteen-foot monument made of Lake

Superior and mine rocks and four new brass plaques and flagpole turned the clock back to 1935, when the monument was first dedicated.

Among those helping out were school children, fifty Army ROTC Cadets from the Calumet High School and Gipp's alma mater. Many turned out to haul rocks from Lake Superior's shore for the monument. The Superior Block Company gave the committee a good deal on brick and sent them to be engraved. Moyle Development Inc., gave Vairo and his two colleagues a concrete mason to build the new monument.

$25,000 was needed to complete the project, with the village donating $3,100.00. The brick sales went well.

Since Laurium is a residental community, it has many churches. One of the most well-known is St. Paul's Evangelical Lutheran Church, formerly known as the German Lutheran Church, located at Second and Tamarack Streets. The parish was organized in 1879, and for two years the members met in various homes before buying a lot on Scott Street in Calumet in 1881 for the construction of a church. In 1899, the Calumet and Hecla Mining Company asked the congregation to vacate the Calumet lot. Earlier, the congregation had been given two lots, at Second and Tamarack Streets, and on one a parson-son was erected. A lot across the street was purchased and work began immediately on the new church. The cornerstone for the new building was laid in June of 1899. Dedication of the new building was on the Sunday before Christmas in 1899. In 1902 a pipe organ was presented to the congregation by Ernst Bollman, and a carved altar and pulpit were purchased for the church in 1904. This church is an architectural example of that late Victorian period.

From 1881-1928 parochial school classes were taught, the latter twenty-two years of this time in the building now known as the VFW building on First Street of Laurium. In 1929, due largely to the Depression, the now VFW building was sold to the village.

Among the most prized possessions of St. Paul's is its pipe organ. Since its installation in 1902, this organ has been used for religious services. This author, when living across the street from St. Paul's, can pleasantly remember the organ music and singing that came from the open windows of that church. The Rev. Frank Schultz was often the organist, and while Practicing, would provide the neighborhood with a beautiful organ concert. We would sit on our front steps and listen to him play. Two new ranks of pipes were added to the organ in 1979 in preparation for the one hundred year centennial celebration.

This congregation observed its one-hundred birthday on August 11, 12, and 13th of 1979. The interior of the church had been repainted and carpeted for the centennial celebration. The Rev. Frank Schultz, the most recent past pastor was the speaker while Harvey L. Gustafson of Ely, Minnesota,

Saint Paul's Evangelical Lutheran Church, Laurium

was the guest organist. Many other pastors attended the centennial celebration.

Pastors who served St. Paul's are the following: F. B. Arnold, 1880-1889; C. Engelder, 1890-1893; J. Huchthausen, 1894-1904; A. Kuring, 1904-1909; A. Bartling, 1909-1918; A. Sommers, 1918-1928; A. S. Lucas, 1928-1941; W. E. Maas, 1942-1955; Walter F. Biel, 1956-1957; Frank J. Schultz, 1958-1976; Frederick P. Buth, 1977-1981; and Walter R. Leininger, from 1981 to present. The Rev. Frank Schultz served the longest term, nine-teen years.

In 1920, St. John's Church in Hubbell became a "sister" church, the Laurium church pastor also conducting services there.

The Apostolic Lutheran Church of Laurium is located on the corner of Tamarack and Third Streets. It was founded on October 10, 1929, when the congregation purchased the church known as the Swedish Lutheran Church which had been constructed in the 1890's. The Apostolic Lutherans formally dedicated the church on November 3, 1929. Sunday School had opened a week earlier for ninety-eight students.

Members of the first board of trustees were Edward Keisu, Charles Johnson, Charles Aittama, Charles Palosaari, John Tuira, John Hookana, John Jokela, Matt Oinas, and Herman Ervast. Shortly after, the Rev. John Oberg was elected to be the first pastor. He later was elected President

The Apostolic Lutheran Church of Laurium

of the Apostolic Lutheran Church of America, of which the members were affiliates. During a portion of 1934 and 1935, the Rev. Viljo Jamsa, a native of Finland, assisted him. In 1942, the Rev. W. A. Karvonen was elected to serve as pastor and served for thirty years. For a period of several years, the Rev. Andrew Mickelsen of Hancock assisted him at communion services. The Rev. Rodney Johnson was elected pastor in 1983.

The Daily Mining Gazette reported on Friday, January 16, 1981, that this congregation was holding a dedication service to celebrate the near comple- tion of a fuel-saving renovation project that had been started during the summer of 1980. The church had a new roof, new cedar siding, and thermo pane glass over its cathedral windows. Russell Lepisto of Bootjack was the project designer as well as a member of the church congregation. He believed it was a mistake that some congrega- tions replaced their churches with new ones when the present ones could be renovated.

They retained the old cathedral windows by installing new thermo pane windows on the exterior. They also removed the old entrance and high stairway, replacing it with a new narthex which had two landings, provid- ing easier access to the sanctuary for the older members. This area includes a fellowship hall and five rooms for Sunday School students. Through this renovation project, the congregation believed they could save fifty percent on their fuel costs.

The Rev. Rodney Johnson, pastor, said renovation also involved other areas of the church. The former parsonage was dismantled and the lumber salvaged. A pastor's study was added to the church in that area. The organ had also been relocated from the balcony to an alcove in the front of the church. The kitchen had been remodelled with a new floor, ceiling, new lights, counter top, and pantry area. The church's heating system was changed from steam to hot water, a change which lowered fuel consumption immediately.

The special dedication involved the Rev. George Wilson of New York Mills, Minnesota, the Rev. Arvo Onermaa of Hancock, and the resident pastor, the Rev. Rodney A. Johnson who makes his home in the Traprock Valley, Lake Linden.

The Methodist Episcopal Church was formally organized on Sunday, October 16, 1898, when the society of the Laurium Methodist Church meeting took place. Forty-two men and women enrolled as charter members of the church. The first pastor, the Rev. H. A. Leeson, arrived before the congregation had a church. His pay was fixed at $75.00 per month.

The first board of stewards were Joseph J. Paull, Edwin Mills, John Kneebone, William Odgers, John Knowles, Edward Goninan, Richard Karkeek, and James Burgan. The first trustees were E. T. Daume, Charles Ellis, J. A. BeVier, John Prisk, and Thomas E.

Bawden. Mrs. Alec Bradburn was the first president of the Ladies Aid Society, R. H. Champion was superintendent of the Sunday School, and Daume was treasurer of the church. Services were held in Munro Hall, above a saloon and restaurant. On December 31, 1898, the church membership was seventy with a Sunday School enrollment of two-hundred and fifty-three students.

The lots for the church were purchased in November of 1899 for $2,000. Beginning in the summer of that year the Laurium town hall became the service quarters for the next thirty months.

According the The Daily Mining Gazette published on August 2, 1902, the exact date of the dedication of the new church had not yet been set. However, the work on the building had progressed so far that the church people were beginning to know as to when the church would be completed and were planning their dedication services. The dedication preacher had already been secured, namely the J. W. Powell of Buffalo who was recognized as the most powerful layman in the Methodist Episcopal Church in this country.

The church people had granted the contract for the heating plant to the Carlton Hardware Company. There were a number of bids for the job, but that of the local firm was the most satisfactory to the trustees. The contract for the seats had been awarded to the Manitowoc Seating company of Wisconsin.

The Methodist Episcopal Church of Laurium

The pews were heavy, quarter-sawed oak, and the church has a seating capacity for four-hundred people.

The congregation did not let a contract for the building, but had the work done under the direction of A. H. Rickman. It was reported on August 2, 1902, that so far they had managed to get along very well financially. The framework for the building had been completed and most of the brick work for the front was up. The plasterers were to start the next Monday or Tuesday and the completion of the church was simply a matter of a few weeks away.

On June 8, 1902, the corner stone of the church was laid and on October 19, 1902, the church was dedicated. The total construction cost was approximately $14,000. At that time there were one-hundred fifty-five members and four-hundred in the Sunday School. The pipe organ was a gift of Mrs. C. E. Moyle and was dedicated on March 4, 1906. According to Calumet's Evening Journal, the congregation purchased the lot adjoining the church on July 11, 1906. This lot was purchased through the agency of David Armit from Albert Buneufant, with the consideration being $2,850.00. This provided the church with a fine site for any addition which might be needed in the future. Once the new building was erected, the membership almost doubled, and on every Sunday the building was filled to its utmost capacity.

Enlarging the church to seat one-thousand people was completed on July 18, 1909. With a new heating plant, the renovating cost was near $10,000. In the 1920s, however, people began leaving the Copper Country area and membership suffered, so changes and adjustments were made. In 1936, the church became the First Methodist Church following the uniting of the M. E. Churches north and south with the Methodist Protestant Church. In 1968 when the original tower was removed, it became the first United Church with the E. U. B. Church.

Now known as the Laurium United Methodist Church, they celebrated their 100th anniversary on Saturday, June 27, 1998. The congregation celebrated with an Open House which was conducted from 1 to 4 p.m., and the public was welcomed. A Hymn Sing and reminiscing at 7 p.m. was followed by a fellowship and later refreshments were served.

Members were reminded that many changes were completed in the 1920's when the building was expanded to seat 1,000 people which it frequently did during the evening service. As the local copper mines closed, many people were forced to leave the area in the early twenties and many parishioners were lost. The remaining people closed the galleries, the south wing and the east end of the building.

According to a newspaper article published on June 27, 1998, the sanctuary now seated about 150 people and the church had 129 members with 42 attending Sunday School.

Pastors who served the Laurium
United Methodist Church are listed as
follows:

H. Addis Leeson --------	1898 -	1903
William E. Marvin ------	1903 -	1908
William M. Ward --------	1908 -	1911
M. H. Eldred -----------	1911 -	1913
Aaron Baux Sutcliffe ---	1913 -	1918
Lewis Keast ------------	1918 -	1923
Harry Ernest Smith -----	1923 -	1924
Aaron Mitchell ---------	1924 -	1928
George G. Hicks --------	1928 -	1931
Herbert Carroll Cooley -	1931 -	1934
John J. Pacey ----------	1934 -	1944
Milton M. Bank ---------	1944 -	1945
Dean W. Parker ---------	1945 -	1947
Harold A. Nessel -------	1947 -	1951
Harold W. Diehl --------	1951 -	1955
John N. Grenfell -------	1955 -	1960
N. Ralph Guilliat ------	1960 -	1965
W. Edward Tillitz ------	1965 -	1967
J. Harold Wallis -------	1967 -	1969
Alan W. DeGraw ---------	1969 -	1972
James E. Tuttle --------	1972 -	1975
Harold J. Slater -------	1975 -	1978
R. Wayne Hudson --------	1978 -	1983
Dennis N. Paulson ------	1983 -	1987
Pamela J. Scott --------	1987 -	1989
Jack E. Johnston -------	1989 -	1992
Mary L. Rose -----------	1992 -	1994
Christine Bohnsack -----	1994 -	2000
Richard Brown ---------	2002 -	Present
Robert A. White -------	2002 -	Present

Pastors White and Brown serve a
four-church charge, those being
Mohawk/Ahmeek, Calumet, Lake Linden and
Laurium.

The Lake Linden Avenue Gospel Hall was built in 1915 and 1916.

The Lake Linden Avenue Gospel Hall was first the church of the Finnish Methodists who built it in 1915. According to the Keweenaw Miner published November 4, 1916, the Finnish Church was just being completed. Carpenters were at work on the church located on Lake Linden Avenue, and it was expected that it would be completed before Christmas. Services had been conducted regularly by the pastor, Reverend K. A. Nurmi, and the work would not interfere with the regular services. The church was thirty-two by forty-four feet, two stories in height, and would be a fitting place of worship for the rapidly growing congregation.

According to a Daily Mining Gazette article dated August 19, 1983, this building was sold in 1951 to the present Christians who gather there, according to one of its members, who preferred anonymity. We try to stick to the scriptural language of the Bible," he said. "We believe there are people who are born again and are saved by the grace of God. We believe Christians constitute the church, and we believe if any member has the gift to speak the word he is qualified to preach it."

The hall, which has been kept in repair has seating for about one hundred people. It is carpeted, gas heated, and has kitchen facilities. Three speakers alternate in delivering the messages from the pulpit. Services, Sunday School, and adult Bible study are conducted.

The Laurium Gospel Tabernacle (now called the Northwoods Christian Assembly), was founded in 1942 by a missionary, Martha Ramsey, who was unable to return to her mission in Africa because of the war. She was a Minnesota native living in Hancock at the time. When she returned to Africa in 1945, the Reverend Aaron W. Peterson of Marquette became the church pastor. Succeeding pastors have been Henry Jauhiainen, Robert Osterlund, Gordon Scott, Emil Carlson, Delbert Grandstrand, and Gerald Wexelberg.

According to Pastor Grandstrand, this church was purchased in 1943. It had been the old Wesley Methodist Church on the corner of Fifth Street in Laurium. It was remodeled at the time it was purchased. Before the official church opening on September 7, 1944, a new roof, interior decorating, new lighting, a remodeled basement, and a new front entrance were completed.

Delegates from Duluth, Marquette and other locations were present for the church dedication, the Reverend's E. C. Erickson and G. J. Flokstra of Duluth were the dedicating speakers. Others present were the Reverend's H. A. Gross of Chicago, Olaf Bakken and members of his congregation of Marquette, Emil Carlson of Minong, Wisconsin, and Evangelist and Mrs. Arthur Rupp of Colfax, Wisconsin. On February 13, 1945, a service to incorporate the Pentecostal church was held, with twenty-one members present.

It was incorporated under the name of Laurium Gospel Tabernacle.

Elected pastor was Aaron W. Peterson; elders were J. C. Rasmussen and Peterson; trustees, Arthur Wickstrom, C. A. Busch, and Laurence Blau; and Sunday School Superintendent, Arthur Wickstrom.

On September 22, 1972, a dedication service marking the completion of a major remodeling program was held. The remodeling, which began in July 1971, included a twenty by twenty-four foot addition in which was built the pastor's study, a nursery, and a new church entrance. The church had also been carpeted throughout, the sanctuary paneled and painted, and new kitchen facilities and a new furnace installed.

The Daily Mining Gazette announced on September 20, 1985 that this church had a new name. According the the Reverend Kenneth Toth, church pastor, the church's name had been changed to the Northwoods Christian Assembly two months before. They were also planning to move to a three-acre parcel of property on U.S. 41 south of Calumet near the entrance to the Golf Course Road. Reverend Toth said the main reasons for the move were space and location.

Many of Laurium's older citizens will remember the Finnish Episcopalian Church. It seems that in September of 1914, the old protestant church located at the Cliff Mine had been purchased by the Finnish Episcopal Congregation of

The Northwoods Christian Assembly is the former Laurium Gospel Tabernacle.

Laurium and the structure moved to a
new location between Florida and
Iroquois Steet. The building was
throughly remodeled and an addition was
erected. The foundation which measured
thirty-two by forty feet was laid by
contractor Charles Johnson.

The Episcopal congregation had
orginally planned to build a new church
and a considerable sum of money had
been raised for the purpose. With the
acquisition of the Cliff edifice, a
large part of the fund would be saved
and a substantial building would be
erected as well.

This Cliff Church was one of the
oldest edifices in the Copper Country,
having been erected more than fifty
years before, and considerable local
history hinged about the building. As
were most of the buildings erected in
the old days, the church was a strong,
substantial structure; and despite the
long years it had been unoccupied, it
was well preserved. Its beams and
sills were of pine, hewed from the
forests that surrounded the community,
and all the lumber could be utilized.

By November of 1914, all the the
materials had been moved and the church
was ready for occupancy by the
congregation.

Laurium once had two large banks.
The first, the State Savings Bank of
Laurium, commenced doing business in
November of 1897. It is said that any
body of men with capital and desire
could start a bank, but the progress

This picture of the Savings Bank of Laurium was extracted from "A Souvenir In Photogravure of the Upper Peninsula of Michigan," printed by W. E. Steckbauer, Photographer, Calumet, Michigan and published in 1900.

they made depended on their knowledge of sound financiering and the confidence of the people. This bank started with a capital of $50,000, and during the next twenty years it had been necessary to increase the capitalization twice. In 1901, $25,000 was added to the original capital and in 1907 a like sum. Earned surplus and profit meant sound banking and every bank was seeking both. The State Saving Bank had $125,000 in that fund.

Progress made by the bank had been due, in large measures, to the successful business men in Laurium who managed its affairs. In April of 1916, the Keweenaw Miner reported that no financial institution in the Copper Country had a more efficient staff or officers or representative citizens on the board of directors. They were identified with many of the leading business concerns of the Upper Peninsula, widely known and in touch with all people of all classes.

The officers and directors of this bank, located on the corner of 405 Hecla Streets, were Johnson Vivian, President; William H. Thielman, Vice-President; James T. Fisher, Cashier; and Edward P. Bast, Assistant Cashier. Directors included Johnson Vivian, J. P. Peterson, William H. Thielman, W. H. Faucett, F. S. Carlton, James A. Torreano, and James Fisher.

Laurium's second bank was the First National Bank of Laurium. It was organized on February 18th, 1907, and

The First National Bank of Laurium, in 1907, was located at the southwest corner of Hecla and Third Streets. Courtesy of the First of American Bank - Copper Country, Calumet and Laurium, Michigan.

located at 301 Hecla Street. The
bank's first capital stock was
$100,000, and because of sound banking,
conservative business methods, and the
people's friendship, no change was made
in this. In April of 1916, the bank
had an earned surplus of $50,000. This
bank had over four-thousand open
accounts to keep its bookkeepers busy.

The men who had made the First
National Bank one of the fastest
growing houses of finance in the Copper
Country were among the best known
business and mining men living in the
Upper Peninsula. William J. Reynolds
of Laurium was the President; Alexander
Levin and Frederick S. Easton of
Calumet were Vice Presidents and J. P.
Paton was the cashier.

Some of the directors were these:
Thomas E. Bawden of Laurium, a general
merchandiser; Richard C. Blight of
Eagle River, fuze manufacturer; Fred S.
Eaton of Calumet, chief clerk of C & H;
Frank H. Haller of Osceola, Superinten-
dent of the Osceola Consolidated Mining
Company; George Hall of Laurium, pres-
ident of the Calumet Brewing Company,
Alexander Levin, a Calumet jewler;
Peter McCelland, of Calumet, supply
clerk at C & H; William J. Reynolds of
Laurium, meats and provisions; and
Michael Richetta of Laurium, merchant
and treasurer of the Italian Mutual
Fire Insurance Company.

Others included Dr. C. H. Rodi of
Calumet, who was director of the
German-American Loan and Trust Company;

C. E. L. Thomas of Calumet, from the
Thomas Insurance Agency; and Vincent
Vairo of Laurium, who was president of
the Italian Mutual Fire Insurance
Company.

Besides the bank which occupied
the ground floor, the Superior Pharmacy
was located to the left of the bank in
the same First National Bank Building.
Its proprietors were Dr. Donald K.
MacQueen and Tony W. Sibilsky. Dr.
MacQueen, a physician, also had his
office on an upper floor. Other
offices upstairs included that of M. E.
O'Brien, general agent for the Northwestern Mutual Life Insurance Company
of Wisconsin; the Calumet Real Estate
Company; and David Armit, general
insurance, steamship, and real estate
agent; and justice of the peace and
notary public. There were also two
lawyers and a dentist with offices in
this building.

Many years later, on the 28th of
November, 1928, through a merger, the
Laurium Branch of the Merchants and
Miners Bank came into effect. The two
earlier banks now became part of
Laurium's history. This bank was one
of the largest of five banks serving
northern Houghton County and Keweenaw
County, with the main bank being
located in downtown Calumet.

It seems that the Merchants and
Miners Bank acquired the assets of the
State Savings Bank in 1928 and a few
years later it assumed the assets of
the First National Bank and moved its
Laurium office to this new site across

the street. The branch continued to serve the village from this new location until September 23, 1968, when it moved to its newly built quarters at 400 Hecla Street.

The now vacated building, located on lots 24 and part of lot 23 at 301 Hecla Street, was offered to the village fathers. They accepted the building and property as one of the largest gifts that had ever been provided, as this had an estimated replacement cost of over a million dollars. The building had been constructed in 1910 and was reportedly as sturdy as the day it was built.

The new bank constructed on the corner of 400 Hecla Street replaced several old business, one being Alden Steck's greenhouse and the Stop and Shop Grocery previously owned by Joseph B. Latoski. The new branch building was forty by fifty feet, of steel and brick construction, and provided four teller windows, with approximtely six-hundred safety deposit boxes, ample parking space, a drive-up window, and a community room.

The bank's officials felt that this new building and location were necessary for these public conveniences and increased efficiency since the old building site provided no parking facilities, no possibility for a drive-up window, and a building which was too large and ineffecient.

The bank people believed that the new facility would bring a nominal

increase in deposits, and that the
earnings would remain constant in spite
of the increased amount paid on
interest deposits. Of course, in 1967,
this was all based on the fact that the
Calumet and Hecla Copper Mining Company
had just recently announced plans for
the development of a large deposit of
copper. Everyone believed that this
would mean more employment as well as
insuring a long life for Laurium.

On June 6, 1983, the Merchant and
Miner's Bank ceased to exist when it
was renamed First of America. Several
years before this date, twenty-eight
banks in two-hundred different
locations all belonged to to the same
holding company but were all under
different names. However, on June 6th,
all the banks changed to the same name.
Laurium's branch became known as First
of America Bank - Copper Country. At
this time Glenn A. McCabe was the
assistant vice president and this
branch's manager. Mr. McCabe retired
from this position on January 1, 1986,
after twenty-five and a half years in
the banking business.

Since Laurium is named after the
Laurium Copper Company, some data
pertaining to the company will be
provided here. An article in the
Native Copper Times, Lake Linden's
newspaper dated August 16, 1898,
states: "In building the two new
streets in Laurium's latest addition,
it became necessary to blast some rock
in order to make the roadbed level.
After a few blasts had been made, it

was discovered that a vein of copper, the same on which the Kearsarge Mine is operating, was laid open. The vein is of a very promising nature and it is rumored that actual mining operations will be begun on the lode by the Laurium Company next spring."

Alvah L. Sawyer stated in his book A History of the Northern Peninsula of Michigan and Its People said that the Laurium Copper Company was a subsidiary of the Calumet and Hecla. Its lands originally consisted of six-hundred forty acres lying east of the Calumet and Hecla tract. From this amount a triangular piece of about sixty-five acres carrying both surface and mineral rights was sold, many years ago, to the Calumet and Hecla Mining Company, and some two- hundred fifty acres of surface rights have since been sold in the form of building lots in the village of Laurium. As mineral rights were reserved, this gave the company holdings of approximately three-hundred twenty-five acres of surface rights and five-hundred seventy-five acres of mineral rights. The village of Laurium lies between two north shafts, numbers twenty and twenty-one.

Nothing much seems to have been accomplished in the line of copper mining, however, Horace J. Stevens reported in 1904 in his book The Copper Handbook that the Laurium Mining Company lands, adjoining the Calumet and Hecla were of doubtful mineral value, but in good demand for building purposes. Active mining developments

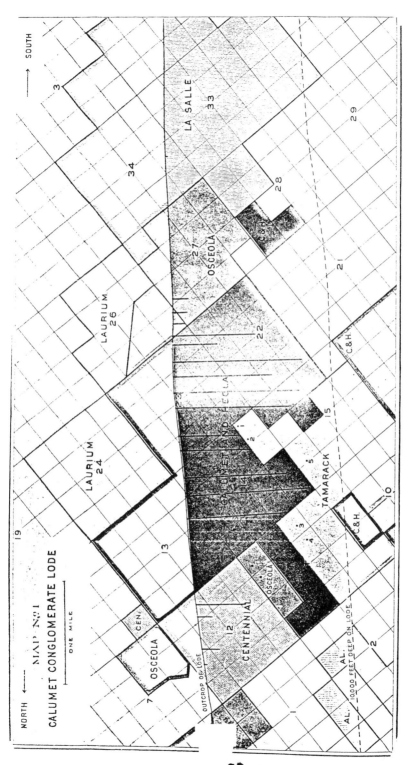

CALUMET CONGLOMERATE LODE

MAP No. 1

ONE MILE

NORTH

SOUTH

were commenced on this property in August of 1909.

According to the annual report for 1909, a shaft about two-thousand two-hundred feet from the southwest corner of Section twenty-six had been sunk four-hundred fifty-six feet. This shaft was located with a view to sinking a second shaft about two-thousand six-hundred feet to the north. The equipment at this shaft consisted of a rock house of about six-hundred tons daily capacity, a boiler house with one large Belpaire boiler, an engine house with small engine and compressor, and a dry house.

In December of 1910, a report was issued to the stockholders of the Laurium Mining Company. The plan was to form a consolidated corporation consisting of the Seneca Mining Company, the Ahmeek Mining Company, the Allouez Mining Company, the Osceola Consolidated Mining Company, the Centennial Copper Mining Company, the Laurium Mining Company, the Tamarack Mining Company, the La Salle Copper Company, the Superior Copper Company, and the Calumet and Hecla Mining Company. The name of the consolidated corporation was to the Calumet and Hecla Mining Company.

Like the other copper mining companies, the Laurium was in trouble and could only survive only through consolidation. The report stated that the cost of repurchasing the surface of section 24 (which had been sold many years before), in order to sink a shaft and erect the necessary equipment, and the small area on the Kearsarge load, at that point made it impossible to mine this ground independently at a profit. If values existed in the ground they could be profitably secured only in connection with the Calumet and Hecla operations on this lode.

Development work on the Kearsarge lode in section twenty-six led to the belief that operations would be profitable if conducted there on a large scale. The territory adjacent to the company's shaft, however, was not large, and at a depth of about two-thousand five hundred feet the shaft would run into Osceola ground. Under the consolidation, the shaft became available for mining the ground of both companies, so that underground operations could be conducted economically and with no greater cost for equipment than would be necessary for Laurium alone. To the south of the shaft the ground adjacent to the La Salle property could be more economically mined through the Number One La Salle shaft. Thus the Laurium Mining Company became a part of the well known Calumet and Hecla Mining Company.

The community of Laurium lost Tebor's Store located on Hecla Street, the village's main street, on May 17, 2002. After its 100-year old history, owner Claire Orr, who worked every day except on Christmas Day for thirty-two years, said it was "just time to close shop. I'm eighty years old and figure now would be a good time to retire."

Business was not bad, as the little village store carried many of the basic grocery staples, beverages, and was a popular spot for kids, since she carried a large selection of candy. Orr said that the store's closing was a sad day for her and that she would miss all the fine people, especially the little ones. "I'm going to miss their hugs," she said.

Another well known corner grocery store in Laurium is Pat's Market which is located on Hecla Street, and was named after the original owner whose last name was Patsloff. He came to the area as a copper miner who then opened the store in the early 1900s.

Then Marge Miller and her brother Art Miller owned the store. Later Rosalie Marson owned and operated the market for thirty-three years.

Ater the store was closed during the summer of 2002, it was reopened by Bill Miller, owner of Miller's Recreation bowling. He said "It was just time to do something different. I've been working in the bowling alley for forty years and this is something new to try." He purchased the business in June and opened the newly remodeled business on September 30, 2002. Miller said that the people in the area really support this store at the northern end of town, since he has the largest food stock in the area, with a little bit of everything.

Pat's Market carries a broad selection of ice cream, pizzas and

candy. The four aisles are stocked
with pop, canned goods, cereal, laundry
products, pet food, snack food, picnic
supplies and dairy products. He also
added a Deli-Express serving hot
sandwiches, coffee, tea and has a
cappuccino bar.

Many older residents remember
Harvey's Bottling Works. The building
located on Florida Street was built for
Richard T. Harvey in July of 1897.
During its heyday, Harvey's "pop" was a
famous drink in the area north of
Dollar Bay. It was distributed no
further south because the citizens of
Laurium, Calumet, Lake Linden, Hubbell
and vicinity, and those towns in the
Keweenaw County kept consuming it as
fast as it was made. The firm provided
work for four employees.

One of Harvey's best sellers was
the lemon soda. "It was used widely
for medicinal purposes and was shipped
to the Mayo Clinic and as far as
Arizona," George Harvey reported.

When Harvey's first operated, the
firm had to bottle its beverage with
wooden corks attached to wires. As
they were made available, rubber caps
with zinc tops were used. These were
followed by crown caps. "We had one of
the first crown foot power cappers from
the Crown Cork and Seal Company of
Baltimore, Maryland," Harvey reported.
"We could put out about two hundred
cases of pop a day with it."

Harvey's Bottling Company at first
had storage space on the basement
floor, the bottling shop on the second

and the Harvey home on the third. "We had eight bedrooms because we had eight children," Harvey said. The attic was used to house bottling stuff such as caps and labels.

In 1944, Harvey gave his company to Walter Opland and Clarence Goulette, company employees. In 1963, Goulette retired the business. For years, Harvey's supplied public saunas in the area with Saturday night pop. Harvey's gingerale, iron brew, lemon soda, orange, grape, cherry, strawberry, rock and rye, raspberry and root beer were always selections in the case.

George Harvey, son of the founder, said that Harvey's was the last bottling works in the State of Michigan that operated on the firm's name. Other firms used the name of the beverage, but Harvey's sold its own trade-mark.

The building was purchased by Walter Makela in 1965, two years after the company closed its doors, for the lumber to be used for other building usage.

In July of 1915, Laurium obtained a knitting mill. It had an original output of six-hundred pair of hose a day. According to the Keweenaw Miner Steven Stiglich of Laurium, who had work with this line in Milwaukee, was the proprietor. He installed ten machines, each with a capacity of sixty pair of hose a day. Employment was given to ten girls who were paid good wages, and a high-class product was turned out. All grades of cotton and wool hose for men were manufactured at

The Harvey Bottleing Works was established in 1898,
making lemon, orange, cherry, rock and rye and
cream sodas. Located on 105 South Streets,
Clarence Goulette and Walter Opland were owners.

the beginning. Later women's high
grade cotton, wool, and silk hostery,
sweaters, sweater-coats, and other knit
good, were added.

A year later, in November of 1916,
the S. & S. Knitting Company announced
that the manufacturing of a new product
- namely, heavy wood wool shirts for
men - would start. There had been a
big demand for this article, and the
salesman declared a steady market would
be assured. This shirt was especially
suited to the needs of woodsmen,
teamsters, and men employed out of
doors for the greater part of the time.

Although orginally a knitting
company, the manufacturing of other
garments, principally house dresses for
women, school dresses, kimonas, night
dresses, waists, and undergarments,
etc., was given as much attention by
the company as the making of knitted
goods, and the output was just as
large. With additional machinery, the
knitting department also had grown very
satisfatorily, and the demand had
increased to such an extent that it was
dificulty to keep up with requests for
these products.

This company closed for a year and
reopened in July of 1921 under the
management of Joseph Stiglich, resuming
operations at its old building on the
corner of Fourth and Osceola Streets.
The machinery had been reinstalled and
twenty girls were employeed, most of
the same employees as before.
Approximately one thousand eight
hundred fifty pairs of socks were
turned out daily. This knitting plant

LAURIUM BASE BALL TEAM, CHAMPIONS OF THE UPPER PENINSULA 1915

THE LAURIUM BASE BALL TEAM, CHAMPIONS OF THE UPPER PENINSULA, 1915.

Top row: Aino Aho, pitcher; Joseph Savinni, catcher; Peter Murphy, pitcher; and Steven Shager, right field.

Middle row: Clement Crase, second base and Captain; Stanley Skinner, official scorer and secretary; and Matt Nicolal, first base, manager and treasurer.

Bottom row: Edward Tobola, left field; George Oliver, third base; Kurick Tornquist, short stop, and George Gipp, center field.

This postcard was published through the courtesy of Mrs. Isabelle Monette of Lake Linden.

already had a contract for
five-hundered and seventy-six thousand
pairs of socks for the Elkis Hosiery
Company of Philadelphia.

This author has not been able to
obtain any other data pertaining to
this knitting mill. If you have any
other information or pictures, please
let me know and I will update this
article in the next volume.

Work on the plant for the Calumet
Gas Company began in June of 1906.
Built in Florida Location, the trenches
for the laying of the gas mains started
on Friday afteroon, June 15, 1906, on
Elm Streets between Sixth and Seventh
Streets in Calumet. The mains were
installed in this manner so that when
the company started active operations
it would not be necessary to tear up
the streets. Enginner Frank D. Moses
was already working on the gas plant.

According to Mr. Moses they would
be supplying customers in about three
months, so that there was no reason
whatever for the company not furnishing
the illuminant by October 7th, at the
latest.

According to an article in the
Daily Mining Gazette, information
provided by Engineer Moses stated that
the cost of installing the gas system,
was well within the amount of stock
sold by the company. In fact, it was
believed that by the time that the
company was supplying gas, less than
two-thirds of the money in the treasury
would have been expended.

The Peninsular Gas Company began tearing down one its older buildings constructed in 1906. It had originally been part of the old gas plant, later, it became a warehouse until the new garage was built behind it in 1982.

The work of installing a gas system in Red Jacket (Calumet) and Laurium would be considerably less than that of doing work in the Portage Lake towns where it was necesssary in some places to go through solid rock. With one or two exceptions, the mains in Red Jacket would be laid in soft ground. The plant itself was being built in Florida Location on five lots which the company had purchased sometime before.

The fact that Red Jacket was already working its pavement would not interfere in the least with the plans of the Calumet Gas Company. Provisions had been made for the installation of more temporary mains in streets and where alleys cross and which were to be paved. With this taken care of, the gas company could confine its entire attention to the installation of mains in the alleys of Red Jacket as well as in Laurium any time that summer when convenient.

Citizens from Laurium would have the first opportunity of using gas, for it was the plan of the company to start its mains to that village first. As soon as it was possible to manufature gas, the illuminate would be piped on to the consumers in Laurium, and then the work would be extended to Red Jacket.

The work was done so that it was possible to extend mains without interrupting the service, and by this method part of the cost of installing the mains could be paid for from profits made from gas manufacturing.

The plant had a capacity of one-hundred-thousand cubic feet per day. The machinery would be of such a nature that additions providing for a larger capacity could be readily added with but little trouble and expense.

The franchise which was given the Calumet Gas Company by both Red Jacket and Laurium provided that the mains should be laid whenever possible in the alleys. The company would confine itself therefore to the alleys alone, except when it was necessary to cross a street. If this had to be done where a street was already paved, it was believed that the company would resort to tunneling below the pavement rather than taking the chance of not getting the street surface back in as good condition as it was before the work started.

There were scores of people in both Red Jacket and Laurium who were anxiously awaiting the time when they would be able to use gas. For both illuminating and cooking purposes, gas was popular, and there was but little doubt that as soon it was introduced into the area the capacity of the gas plant would be taxed serving the communities of Laurium, Calumet, and Lake Linden.

The directors of the Calumet Gas Company had given the contract for the installation of the machinery and the building of the plant to Frank D. Moses. The work of digging the trenches was let to George Hall of Wolverine. Marshall, Wells and Company of Duluth supplied the mains. In all, it was expected that the work would represent an outlay of between $50,000 and $60,000.

When the company first started, it operated directly from the gas plant and had approximately twelve miles of steel pipe mains and dresser couplings. The couplings were used in making the pipe joints for all sizes of pipe larger than three inches diameter. Approximately seven miles of this system was discontinued in 1948 and were reconditioned and put back in service during subsequent years. Until 1957 the system was operated at low pressure, but because of the demand for additional gas, conversion was made to intermediate pressure during the summer of 1957 by the addition of house regulators for each customer.

According to newspaper articles, this company was organized early in 1906 as the Calumet Gas Company and in August 20, 1907, as the Calumet Gas and Coke Company. The company was reorganized in 1918. On November 19, 1935, the firm became the Peninsular Utilities Company, and on August 25, 1947, the name was again changed, this time to the Peninsular Gas Company.

Many people still have memories of the Cozy Garden Resturant which was situated on the corner of Hecla Street and Lake Linden Avenue. The razing of this Laurium business in 1974 caused some heartache to those persons who had patronized the place in the early years of its existence. At first the

Friday, August 26, 1983 · · **And the living is easy**

IT WAS PERFECT A perfect summer evening for a concert in the park last night, and the Calumet Community Band obliged with their last concert of the season in Laurium's Daniell Park. (Gazette photo by Felix Fournier)

building was owned by a Mr. Bawden who used it for a general store. Later a Mr. Richman maintained a general grocery store there.

According to the Daily Mining Gazette, the store was then in the managership of Caserio and Massoglia, and a Mr. Ruelle followed with a grocery and meat market. It wasn't until 1928 that the ownership remained stable. It was in that year that James Galetto, who owned the Galetto Bus Line, purchased the building from Mr. Bawden.

He proceeded to make a garage for buses in the rear of the building, and on November 28, 1928, opened an ice cream parlor and lunch room in the front portion. In 1930, Galetto sold the bus line and then remodeled the building again. He had the ice cream parlor enlarged, adding more booths and a dance floor. The upstairs was made into a dining room for private parties and a dance hall. The Cozy Garden was a popular place for its delicious pork barbecues, hamburgers, and various ice cream dishes.

During the Depression years in the 1930's, customers could buy an ice cream sundae or glass of pop for ten cents, or a hamburger and cup of coffee for fifteen cents, and then dance all evening to the music of the juke box. Many a Copper Country resident will fondly recall those past years. Although people of all ages patronized the Cozy Garden, it was especially enjoyed by the teenagers and those in their twenties who came from all parts of Houghton and Keweenaw Counties to meet their friends and enjoy an evening of dancing or a dish of ice cream.

Mr. Galetto passed away on April 14, 1960, and for the next five years the Cozy Garden was managed by his sister, Mrs. Francis (Angie) Schneller who had worked in the Cozy Garden since it opened in 1928. In January of 1965, the building and business was sold by the Galetto estate to Rudolph Kovachich and then the building was purchased by the Hamar-Quandt Company.

The Hamar-Quandt Company continued to use these facilities until May of 1977, when new facilities replaced the smaller store, warehouse and yard. The grand opening took place on May 5, 6 and 7, 1977, after the firm completed its move into a seven-thousand six-hundred square-foot store and a nine-thousand square-foot warehouse adjoining about fifteen-thousand square feet of yard space at the corner of Lake Linden Avenue and Hecla Street.

Edward Hamar was manager at that time and stated that they had the materials for any building project, from footings to the roofing, for the builder, the light commercial contractor and the do-it-yourselfer. The drive-through warehouse has an entrance on Kearsarge Street and an exit on Lake Linden Avenue. This Laurium store replaced the old yard that was located in Calumet.

Among the full lines of building materials that Hammer-Quandt (now 41

Lumber Company) offer are paneling,
wallpaper, kitchen cabinets, electrical
and plumbing supplies, including light
fixtures, bathtubs, vanities and
commodes: ceiling tiles, paints, hardware, tools, windows, doors, siding,
insulation, fireplaces, masonry
products, and dimension lumber.

When one hears of Laurium, one
also thinks of Jukuri's Sauna. This is
the only public sauna in the Houghton
County area and is located on Lake
Linden Avenue in Laurium. It was
established by the late Emil Jukuri in
1950 and later was operated by his son
Lawrence, who then sold his interests
to James Bayles. The public sauna in
Laurium came about after many private
saunas in the Copper Country area were
opened. Some open for public patronage
were later closed due to the death of
the owners and no one wanted the
business.

Emil Jukuri, a Laurium businessman
who operated a service station for many
years, had been accustomed to saunas
since his youth when he lived on a farm
in Traprock Valley. Usually one of the
farm buildings was the farmer's sauna.
When Emil Jukuri saw the need for a
public sauna in Laurium, he had one
built near his service station. It has
served thousands of bathers through the
years.

Although it is a public sauna, it
is not a communal sauna. Each of the
twelve individual saunas is big enough
to accommodate a family, and each has a
changing room and a shower room.

Owner Jim Bayles believes the public sauna is disappearing because "so many people have their own sauna, and, of course, the population is going down." There is another public sauna in Copper Harbor, he said. The traditional Finnish sauna is more than just a hot sweat. It is a ritual, an art done just so. Devotees claim that, in addition to getting you clean, it prevents colds, helps arthritis and backaches, wakes you up, and relaxes and keeps you warm through the long, cold winter nights.

Most customers are of Finnish descent. New arrivals spill into Jukuri's bringing with them subfreezing air that sinks in clouds of white vapor, rolling over the concrete floor of the lounge. Air is hot and humid, a faint promise of what is waiting down the two corridors leading to the saunas. Pipes hiss in the background.

The lounge is almost spartan with metal folding chairs lining the walls. The only amenity is a coffee machine percolating in one corner. Coffee is another Finnish tradition.

It seems that the traditional Finnish sauna starts with a long, slow sweat. Temperature in the sauna room is gradually increased by throwing water on hot rocks, a process which sends up great clouds of steam. Old-time sauna owners heated rocks in wood stoves, which were carefully stoked and banked all day for the evening sauna. The modern sauna uses gas to heat rocks. Most old timers feel that "wood

The Laurium Streetcar Barn. Courtesy of the G. Walton Smith Collection, Lake Linden, Michigan

was a better heat." The average temperature of the units is about one-hundred fifty degrees, and the customers can control the amount of steam they desire.

The first sauna is followed by a cold shower. Some people still just jump in the snow or a nearby lake. They then return, numbed, to the sauna and remain until "it burns your fingernails" or you reach the same color as a cooked lobster. Of course don't try it the first time you try a sauna they warn. Finish with another cold shower to close all of the skin's pores.

In the traditional sauna, cedar branches are used to whip the skin to stimulate circulation. Jukuri's used to provide branches but stopped because the twigs clogged drains. Some customers, undeterred, still bring in their own branches.

Bayles, who purchased the business in 1974, compares his sauna to a sort of community center, as people come like clockwork for their weekly sauna and visit with friends. Winter week-ends are crowded as families come for a sauna. It's busy because it's too cold to use many family farm saunas, so the people come to Jukuri's instead. Many of the customers are the same ones that began coming when the business opened. According to owner Bayles, "Some of these people have been coming for thirty years."

Like public baths, the public sauna is a disappearing institution.

Jukuri's is one of the last public saunas on the Keweenaw Peninsula, a thread of culture that winds back to the Finnish immigrants who brought the sauna here from the old country before the turn of the century.

Jim Bayles did not use flashy advertising or other gimmicks to entice patrons to his business, but it was busy just the same. Bayles had purchased the sauna after looking for a reason to come back home. Although many locales had public saunas, they usually had only a men's room and a women's room, with large public rooms fit for crowds. Of course there were always arguments about it being too hot or not hot enough. The person with the water bucket controlled the temperature.

For that reason Jukuri's put in separate, private saunas complete with showers. Bayles said that fact alone drew customers, particularly those living in apartments with no showers. Many people came with their kids.

Many customers brought their own refreshments along with them to rehydrate after the steam. Some experimental types brought essential oils to add to the water, loofahs and scrubbies for sloughing off dead skin and loads of cream to keep the moisture in after the sauna was over. Going outside in the winter with wet hair was an "instant huivi."

Jukuri's was open from two to ten p.m. on Wednesdays and Fridays; and from noon to 10 p.m. on Saturdays, since those are the traditional Finnish sauna nights. Friday was thrown in for those folks finishing the work week. Bayles turned on the heat for the twelve units about two hours before he opened the doors. It took that long due to the ceramic and concrete surrounding the building holding the cold. It also held the heat, staying warm for a day after he shut down the system.

Jukuri's Sauna closed its doors in September of 1996. When customers drove up to the building, they were dismayed when the "Sauna Today" sign was not out on the sidewalk to greet them. The building's water system had pooped out and it was simply too expensive for Bayles to replace. The gas bills from the Peninsula Gas tar-ditch cleanup surcharges had also put a crunch on the budget, so profits did not come anywhere near to covering expensive repairs.

The well known Captain Thomas H. Hoatson Jr. home is located at 320 Tamarack Street and was built in 1908 at a cost of $50,000.00. Hoatson was the founder of the Calumet and Arizona Mining Company and built the most elegant home in the area.

This mansion includes a third floor 1,300 square foot ballroom, elephant hide wall coverings, and hand-painted murals which witnessed the lively steps of dancers. The third floor also once housed the Hoatson family's servants and the fur closet. The garage had a turn table so the car could be driven in forward, then rotated to point outward. This home

TAMARACK ST., SHOWING CAPT. THOS. HOATSON'S RESIDENCE, LAURIUM, MICH.

was listed in the National Register of Historic Places on December 9, 1994.

This historic structure is now the home of the Laurium Manor Inn, a bed and breakfast inn, owned by David and Julie Sprenger. It is the largest mansion in the western Upper Peninsula with 13,000 square feet and 45 rooms. The Neo-Classic home has ten guest rooms, a ballroom, library, den, parlor, two dining rooms, and a carriage house. Five fireplaces in various rooms illuminate tile, gold leaf and Italian marble. Plaster and silver leaf decorate the music room's cove ceiling.

Unique features include: gilded Elephant hide/leather wall coverings, wall murals, built-in wall size icebox, gilded marble and tile fireplaces, private balcony, and a thousand square feet of tile wrap around porch. Using the original decorator's list unearthed by Hoatson's family, the Sprengers were able to determine how the rooms had looked at one time. They purchased antique furniture to add to the cira-1908 atmosphere. The carriage house has been transformed into a gift shop.

The Norman MacDonald home built in 1906, is located on 305 Tamarack Street. MacDonald, a druggist, was a large investor in the Calumet and Arizona Mining Company. The garage is located in the rear with the chauffeur's quarters above.

This property is now known as the Victorian Hall Bed and Breakfast and is owned by David and Julie Sprenger. The Bed and Breakfast is open all year

LAURIUM MANOR INN

round and is a 34-room brick and sandstone Victorian Mansion. This three-story 7,500 square foot home has six beautifully carved wood burning fireplaces, four in guests rooms, with ornate stain glass windows, original woodwork and elaborate crown moldings. All rooms are furnished in period antiques. It also has an eighty foot long wrap-around porch. The library, parlor and dining rooms are always open to the guests.

Another turn of the century home was built for William Clark in 1898 and is still located at 209 Pewabic Street. In later years it became Thompson's Keweenaw House Bed and Breakfast and was owned by Lorraine and Robert Thompson. The home now supports a shingled top half painted blue, with the lower half painted white. A bronze marker over the front door tells this history.

Since this house was built in 1898, the first thing the Thompsons did was total rewiring, followed by having the plumbing redone. Drywalling most of the house was necessary, since the walls had 98 years of wallpaper. Two new larger windows were installed and restrooms were completed. The kitchen still had its original flooring and when the Thompsons pulled up the tile in other rooms, they found beautiful hardwood flooring that was still in good shape.

The upstairs portion of the house had three bedrooms, a full bathroom, kitchen and living room. The upper-level living room had the original light fixtures, as well as a

Victorian Hall Bed & Breakfast

photo of how the house looked in its earlier days. The bathroom still has the original sink and claw-foot bathtub.

The Thompsons closed their bed and beakfast several years ago and it is now a private home.

The People's Theatre, located at 236 Hecla Street, was well known. It was in October of 1915 when the Laurium Amusement Company purchased the playhouse and enlarged the building. It seems that the business enjoyed by the Peoples' had been such that it was necessary to either secure larger quarters or to have the present building enlarged. The former owners did not desire to do the enlarging, so the lesses purchased the building and doubled the capacity of the building. They realized that the residents would support them as they needed a larger theatre than they had.

This addition would make the building forty feet deeper, the new addition being the full width of the lot and thirty feet high. Contractor James Thielmen had a force of men at work and the proprietor soon had new opera chairs installed. The seating capacity was doubled according to Manager Fisher. The property was centrally located and was but two doors from Laurium's two banks.

When the theatre was closed, a local contractor used it for his business. This too has closed, and at this time the roof has started to cave in.

This old post card showing a service station located on the corner of Fourth and Hecla Street, was provided by Mrs. Isabelle Monette of Lake Linden.

Leo's Drug Store opened on Tuesday, January 15, 1946. It was located on Third Street, in the Boggio building which was formerly occupied by the Salotti Store. The new, modern drug store was owned and operated by Leo J. Nault, a well known local man, who had 28 years experience as a registered pharmacist, and had been employed as a pharmacist by A. W. Sibilsky of Laurium for the past 20 years.

This drug store was modern in every detail and handled a complete line of pharmaceutical supplies. One of the features in the store was the open display of all merchandise, with emphasis placed on having departments for different items such as vitamins, baby supplies, first aid and hosptial needs, and such. The prescription department was semi-open and was in full view of the customers. The fixtures were all in white.

It was on April 29, 1953, that the Leo Drug Store had its grand opening. Extensive renovating had been in progress for ten weeks to house the many departments, the feature of which was the open prescription department. The Crab Orchard stone entrance made it a smart outside appearance. The stone had been imported from Crab Orchard, Tennesee.

A new double entrance was made necessary so the west half of the building could be a gift department. Doors were aluminum with Thermopane glass. New display windows were also of Thermopane glass. Modern fluorescent lamps lighted the smartly decorated interior which housed

This picture of the Copper Range Railroad and equipment was located in Laurium's North end and was found in the Herman Page Collection maintained by the MTU Archives and Copper Country Historical Collection, Michigan Technological University.

departments for vitamins, prescriptions, proprietary medicines, cosmetics, men's toiletries, hair health supplies, bath, stationery and candy.

Employees working in the store during April of 1953, were William C. Cox, RPh; Beatrice Perala, Dorothy Artrip, LaVerne Maatta and Gloria Bishop.

After eight owners,the drug store's last owner was Edward J. Schniderhan, RPh. In 1967, Ed Schneiderhan along with Roy Maki went into business together continuing the tradition of Leo's Drug. Roy retired in 1980, so Ed became the sole owner of the business. The Schneiderhan family had all worked in the stores over the years helping to continue a tradition of personal care and friendly service.

Mr. Schniderhan closed the store in May of 1998, when he sold the inventory to the Keweenaw Memorial Center. Ed set up the pharmacy on the first floor of the hospital and worked there, retiring several years later.

Another business that is now a part of Laurium's history was the Hermann Hardware, which was located at 337 Hecla Street.

Located in the Ruppe building, which was formerly occupied by the Thurner Bakery on Hecla Street, the business was started in 1928 when the Proprietor, Martin Hermann, purchased the Petermann Hardware Store. That business was located in the buildings

P. STATTINE
Painting and Decorating
WALL PAPER, PAINTS
OILS AND VARNISHES

HECLA STREET 324

Laurium, Mich., *Feb 26* 1906.

8598

THE FIRST NATIONAL BANK OF LAURIUM

CAPITAL $100,000. SURPLUS $25,000.

M. E. O'BRIEN, PRESIDENT.
ALEXANDER LEVIN, VICE-PREST.
WILLIAM J. REYNOLDS, VICE-PREST.
J. B. PATON, CASHIER.
D. J. LEVEQUE, ASS'T CASH.

LAURIUM, MICH. May 3rd.,1907.

Calumet Carriage Works,
JOS. HEBERT, PROP.
MANUFACTURER OF AND DEALER IN
Carriages, Buggies and Sleighs
Horse Shoeing and Rubber-Tiring a specialty.

Laurium, Mich., *April 5* 1905

THOMAS BUZZO,
DEALER IN
Lumber, Square Timber, Flat Timber
AND TIES.

Laurium, Mich., ___4___ 190

formerly occupied by the Birch Casino on Hecla Street. The hardware stock was moved to the new location shortly thereafter.

At the time of the move, the plumbing business predominated, the hardware trade having been expanded during the past ten years. Mr. Martin Hermann was a licensed plumber.

In 1938, the hardware store received a contract to install boilers and hot water tanks in the Calumet and Hecla Mining Company homes that were being cut off from mining company furnished steam. About forty-five homes were so converted.

A unique street sign, in the shape of a huge faucet, set off with neon lighting in the evening, had been made over fifty years before by Clarence McFadden in Laurium. It was made sixteen times the size that the Fuller Company made their faucets, and was believed to be the only one of its kind in the country. It was made from galvinized iron in the Peninsula Heating and Plumbing Company Shop. This shop was later the Seppala-McCormack Service Station.

In addition to Mr. Hermann, two plumbers, Joseph Shaltz and Francis Munch, and two clerks, Edward Hepting and Michael J. Richetta were employed. U.S. Solar oil burners and boilers were featured in this store.

After the hardware store closed, the owner of the next door Shawn's Restaurant and Pizzeria purchased the building for its new dining room to cater to large groups of people.

Few residents remember the over 70 year old Standard Oil Company service station that was located on the corner of Lake Linden Avenue and Osceola Street. However, the building remains as originally constructed, and at present serves the Luoma Insurance Agency.

The Standard Oil Company built the station, and after several years serving the citizens of Laurium, was sold to the Spurr Gas Station people.

The Luoma Insurance Agency purchased the building and remodeled it. They moved their offices from Pine Street in Calumet to their new location on November 17, 1980. Serving their clients at this time were Arvo J. Luoma and James P. Bouchey, agents, Sandy Poshak and Lorraine Dextrom as the secretaries. The decision to move to the old Laurium Spur Station was made to allow for more convenient parking and as Jim Bouchey, Luoma's son-in-law said, he felt it was a better location.

Contracts in renovation were let to Palosaari Construction, Dollar Bay Linoleum and Tile Company, Tom Moyle Construction Company, Houghton Black Top, Dale White Electrical and True Value Plumbing.

Then on January 1, 1996, the Luoma Insurance Agency and the Lakeland Insurance Agencies combined their operations. The two agencies then continued to do business at their existing locations, in Laurium and Hubbell.

The new owners, Russ Messner and his son Craig Messner, purchased not only the property and building, but the agency. Russ runs the Laurium office while Craig operates the agency at Tamarack City in Hubbell. Both men are on a full time basis, are licensed agents and are members of the Independent Insurance Agents of Michigan. Thus, they can offer home and auto insurance, and have markets for business insurance, health and life, recreational vehicle including motorcycles, boats, jet skis and snowmobiles.

The residents of Laurium Village and surrounding towns celebrated their 1895 - 1995 year Centennial from Thursday, July 27 through Saturday, August 5, 1995. The events started on Thursday at 7 p.m. with a band concert in Danniell Park with the Stubborn Country band. Friday, starting at 7:30 p.m., found the Centennial Queen Talent Show and coronation cermony being held in the village of Laurium town hall ballroom. On Saturday, the community saw Jimmy B. and the Rockatones at the Bicentennial Arena from 8 p.m. to midnight.

On Wednesay, August 2, a spaghetti dinner was served at the Bicentennial Arena from 3 to 7 p.m. Thursday, starting at 7 p.m. a band concert was held in the Daniel Park with the Windjammers. Friday found the Keweenaw Swing Band at the Bicentennial Arena from 8 p.m. to midnight. They also held a raffle drawing with three $100.00 U.S. saving bonds being given out. The last day, Saturday, August 5, starting at 6 p.m., a centennial parade passed through Laurium. Completing the centennial was the Frankie Yankovic band playing at the Bicentennial Arena from 8 p.m. to midnight.

The Standard Oil Company is now the Lakeland-Luoma Insurance Agency.

SOURCES

The references listed below were used in gathering information to aid in the writing of this publication. Not all of the sources are listed however, as many people of the Copper Country area provided much information.

I especially used the resources of the Michigan Technological University Library and the Daily Mining Gazette, both located in Houghton. I am indebted to Theresa S. Spence, Kay Masters and David H. Thomas of the Michigan Technological University Library for their assistance and the materials they provided from the Library Archives.

PUBLICATIONS

Welcome to the Village of Laurium's 75th Anniversary, 1889-1964, held on July 2, 3, 4. Booklet dated 1964

Welcome to the Village of Laurium's 80th Anniversary, 1889-1969, held on July 1, 11, 12, 13. Booklet dated 1969

Peninsula Portraits, People and Places in Michigan's Upper Peninsula, by Charles Symon, 1980

Michigan Ghost Towns, volume III, Upper Peninsula, by Roy L. Dodge, 1973

Michigan Place Names, by Walter Romig, L.H.D., (not dated)

Laurium Village Centennial, 1895 - 1995, not dated, but the events were from July 27 through August 5, 1995

Houghton County Directory, by R. L. Polk and
   Company, 1901-1902

The Copper Handbook, volume IV, by Horace J.
   Stevens, 1904

Red Metal, The Calumet and Hecla Story, by C.
   Harry Benedict, 1952

Boom Copper, by Angus Murdoch, 1943

The Copper Deposits of Michigan, Professional
   Paper 144, by B. S. Butler and W. S. Burbank,
   1929

NEWSPAPERS

The Keweenaw Miner, Mohawk, Michigan

Calumet News, Calumet, Michigan

The Copper Island Sentinel, Calumet, Michigan

The Daily Mining Gazette, Houghton, Michigan

Portage Lake Mining Gazette, Houghton, Michigan

Native Copper Times, Lake Linden, Michigan

OTHER SOURCES

Donald Julio, Laurium Village Fire Chief

Lucille Kangas, Laurium Village Clerk

Data from the Calumet Public Hospital, Laurium,
   Michigan

Roy Drier Collection, maintained at the Michigan
Technological University Library, Houghton,
Michigan

Michigan History Division, Michigan Department
of State, Administrative Archives, Historical
Sites and Publications, 3423 North Logan Street,
Lansing, Michigan

National Archives Microfilm Publications, National
Archives, Washington, D.C.

Calumet and Hecla Mining Company Collection,
maintained at the MTU Library Archives, Michigan
Technological University, Houghton, Michigan

ADD THIS COPPER COUNTRY LOCAL HISTORY
SERIES TO YOUR PERSONAL LIBRARY

COR-AGO, A LAKE LINDEN MEDICINE COMPANY
First of a local history series

A COPPER COUNTRY LOGGER'S TALE
Second of a local history series

GREGORYVILLE - THE HISTORY OF A HAMLET LOCATED ACROSS
FROM LAKE LINDEN, MICHIGAN
Third of a local history series

WHITE CITY - THE HISTORY OF AN EARLY COPPER COUNTRY
RECREATION AREA
Fourth of a local history series

SOME COPPER COUNTRY NAMES AND PLACES
Fifth of a local history series

THE HISTORY OF LAKE LINDEN, MICHIGAN
Sixth of a local history series

THE HISTORY OF JACOBSVILLE AND ITS SANDSTONE QUARRIES
Seventh of a local history series

THE HISTORY OF COPPER HARBOR, MICHIGAN
Eight of a local history series

THE HISTORY OF EAGLE HARBOR, MICHIGAN
Ninth of a local history series

LAKE LINDEN'S YESTERDAY - A PICTORIAL HISTORY, VOLUME I
Tenth of a local history series

THE HISTORY OF EAGLE RIVER, MICHIGAN
Eleventh of a local history series

JOSEPH BOSCH AND THE BOSCH BREWING COMPANY
Twelfth of a local history series

COPPER FALLS - JUST A MEMORY
    Thirteenth of a local history series

THE CALUMET THEATRE
    Fourteenth of a local history series

EARLY DAYS IN MOHAWK, MICHIGAN
    Fifteenth of a local history series

LAKE LINDEN'S YESTERDAY - A PICTORIAL HISTORY, VOLUME II
    Sixteenth of a local history series

THE KEWEENAW WATERWAY
    Seventeenth of a local history series

A BRIEF HISTORY OF AHMEEK, MICHIGAN
    Eighteenth of a local history series

ALL ABOUT MANDAN, MICHIGAN
    Nineteenth of a local history series

HANCOCK, MICHIGAN, REMEMBERED, VOLUME I
    Twentieth of a local history series

THE SETTLING OF COPPER CITY, MICHIGAN
    Twenty-first of a local history series

LAKE LINDEN'S YESTERDAY - A PICTORIAL HISTORY, VOLUME II
    Twenty-second of a local history series

PAINESDALE, MICHIGAN - OLD AND NEW
    Twenty-third of a local history series

SOME OF THE BEST FROM C & H NEWS - VIEWS, VOLUME I
    Twenty-fourth of a local history series

HANCOCK, MICHIGAN, REMEMBERED - CHURCHES OF HANCOCK,
VOLUME II
    Twenty-fifth of a local history series

OJIBWAY, MICHIGAN, A FORGOTTEN VILLAGE
    Twenty-sixth of a local history series

LAURIUM, MICHIGAN'S EARLY DAYS
    Twenty-seventh of a local history series

DELAWARE, MICHIGAN, ITS HISTORY
    Twenty-eight of a local history series

LAKE LINDEN'S LIVING HISTORY - 1985
    Twenty-ninth of a local history series

SOME OF THE BEST FROM C & H NEWS - VIEWS, VOLUME II
    Thirtieth of a local history series

THE GAY, MICHIGAN, STORY
    Thirty-first of a local history series

EARLY RED JACKET AND CALUMET IN PICTURES, VOLUME I
    Thirty-second of a local history series

LAKE LINDEN'S DISASTROUS FIRE OF 1887
    Thirty-third of a local history series

PHOENIX, MICHIGAN'S HISTORY
    Thirty-fourth of a local history series

FREDA, MICHIGAN, END OF THE ROAD
    Thirty-fifth of a local history series

HOUGHTON IN PICTURES
    Thirty-sixth of a local history series

THE COPPER RANGE RAILROAD
    Thirty-seventh of a local history series

LAC LA BELLE
    Thirty-eight of a local history series

TRIMOUNTAIN AND ITS COPPER MINES
    Thirty-ninth of a local history series

EARLY RED JACKET AND CALUMET IN PICTURES, VOLUME II
    Fortieth of a local history series